GONE

Carmen A. Gray

Gone: A Journey Through Loss

Published by Carmen Gray

GONE

A Journey Through Loss

Carmen A. Gray

Table of Contents

ACKNOWLEDGMENTS

To my baby girl, Destiny Amaris, we have been through incredible pain together, and you are standing strong, baby girl. I am proud of how you chose to live your life to honor your brother's memory. Well done, darling Dee, I know your brother is proud of the young woman you have become. To my parents, Milton and Mattie Mosby, many thanks for the example you set in having an unwavering and uncompromising faith in God. I learned many years ago that "earth has no sorrow that heaven cannot heal." I'd also like to thank my sister, Candace, and brother-in-law, Anthony, for kissing my son on the forehead when he took his last breath and for the limitless support they continue to give. My sister is my rock, and she has been with me through every stage of my grieving process. She has been rescuing me since we were children. Thank you, Sissy.

I'd like to thank my friend, Nicole, who went to the hospital for me in my stead at 3:00 a.m. while I was in Charlotte, North Carolina, and has been through every phase of my son's death with me. I'd like to thank the multitude of family and friends who have taken this journey with me, you know who you are. I am grateful for the sponsors of the LLC foundation and the community members who were my safety net during the worst possible crisis in a mother's life. To my board members, many thanks for allowing me space to grieve while trying to birth out a global vision.

For every person who uttered a prayer for the peace and sanity of my daughter and me through this horrific ordeal of loss, thank you, silent warriors. I am appreciative of my therapists, my psychiatrist, and mental health counselors who saw me and would not let me self-implode. For all of Curtis' tribe, you guys are my heartthrob and Ma Carmen loves each of you for showing up, for aiming to "be great," and for helping me keep Curt's legacy alive. For every news outlet that helped me tell my son's story, many thanks; we still have a lot of ground to cover, so hang in there with me. To all the members of Flagler County School, sheriff's department, fire department, and city and county officials who have taken this journey with me, thank you.

Lastly, if it were not for Curtis' father, I would have never known the joy of birthing my intriguing, beautiful boy. Thank you, Curtis Bernard, for being the necessary connection to produce such a treasure to this world. His legacy will live on. Our son's life has penetrated lives nationally and globally. He knew he would, and so did I.

Finally, I birthed a legend, and I am humbled by it. Thank you, God, for choosing me to be his mother!

Introduction

Hi, I am Carmen Alexis Gray, the mother of two amazing children, Destiny Amaris and Curtis Israel. My son, Curtis Israel Gray, was shot and killed randomly without altercation, a hostile encounter or reason. He lived a purposeful life of service and giving for a community he loved, but his allotted time on earth was for a span of eighteen years. So much life and promise as well—*gone*. The potential of him marrying and fathering children—*gone*. The hope that one day he would bury me in my old age, *gone*—never to be experienced. This disruption of my life impacted my emotional and psychological well-being. Murder is vicious. However, murder without a cause is profoundly immeasurable. The "why" is the worst nightmare any mother or father could ever perceive.

In my tumultuous introduction to grief, I felt as if I would never breathe again; and sadly, the thought was welcoming. I was caught in a tempest, a raging storm, and left to the mercy of the waves of grief, like billows of angry water intent on drowning me in its depths of sorrow for which there aren't words in any language to define or describe the power of that type of grief. Somehow, dear reader, I found a way to stay afloat and not be pulled under by its merciless currents. I discovered a portal of hope—my pen, my beacon—guiding me daily through unchartered territory. My pen kept me from losing my mind, my voice, my hope, and my instinct to thrive.

I pray, dear reader, that you empower yourself through your own journey of grief. May this book of my personal and intimate letters to my son prior to his death and post his life serve as a guide for some type of cognitive therapy that will allow you to journal as well.

I encourage you to purchase the workbook that accompanies this collection of memoirs so you can actively and intentionally define how you will heal. Healing is not something you stumble upon or leave to chance with the notion that time heals all wounds. I have found, in my lifetime, that time perpetuates wounds that go untreated. For example, a broken bone will heal with time; but if improperly set, it will heal incorrectly. I encourage you to proactively invest in your recovery as we journey through loss together.

Grief has no end; it serves as the go-between for the life that remains between parents and the loss of life of their child. It is an invisible connector so that we never forget that the life we birthed or seeded on this earth is not forgotten. The measure of grief that one feels is often a reflection of the measure of love for the one or ones who are gone (if you have lost more than one child).

In this book, you will recognize the stages of grief: denial, anger, bargaining, depression, and acceptance. By the way, there isn't a particular order in these stages, but they continue to cycle like waves on the water. Sometimes, placid and calm. Other times, raging. Analyze them and allow yourself the opportunity for healing post the loss of your child by giving yourself permission to grieve through the entire process. I must confess, I hated the word "process" because in death, it seems ambiguous and indefinite. When used as an admonition, it seems disingenuous when someone kindly tells you to go through "the process" and they themselves cannot relate to the heart-crushing anguish that is inescapable and redefining your life through loss. However, dear reader, you have the power to decide how the death of your child will define you.

Two days before my son passed, he looked me squarely in the eyes and made me promise him I would be great. He said to me earnestly, "Mom, promise me you will be great!" He made me say the words "I will be great." He made me repeat it until he felt satisfied with my commitment in the words. That day, April 11, 2019, my son left me a key to survival. Little did I know that two days later, he would be shot and killed on April 13, 2019. I have lived by that promise through grief. Please borrow it, use it, and commit to it for the sake of your own lost child… "I will be great." Use this book as a guide to help you redefine your life after the death of your child. He or she is indeed gone but never forgotten.

Carmen A. Gray
Proud Momma of Curtis and Destiny

CHAPTER 1

3:37 RENDEZVOUS: FORTY-SIX MINUTES

HEY, baby guy, it's been a while. I drive by the place that staged your death daily; there is no escaping it. I am utterly reminded of the fateful night that snatched your life away from me. So many regrets as I drive by. Forty-six minutes you laid there, waiting for rescue in a parking lot, swarming with the lights of the EMS and Flagler's finest. Why were you detained? There was no sense of urgency in getting you to surgery. Forty-six minutes were drawing you closer to your final timeline on this earth. I know you longed for your mom. I know you thought of all the things you wanted to say to me. I know you remembered all the conversations we had about your departure from this life to the next: "make sure you forgive everyone their trespasses so that yours would be forgiven." I know you felt at peace, and you anticipated death was imminent, yet you were just beginning to live a life of freedom, limitless opportunities, and optimism for a brighter tomorrow. But the clock was ticking, forty-six minutes slipping away, and the urgency of your condition was secondary.

A young Black man out at night, surely, he was up to no good. Why rush him off to safety? He needs to be detained for questioning. A value was placed on your life that night that sealed your fate, cementing your timeline on this earth. Who decided that time should casually slip by for you? Who made the call that more evidence was more valuable than saving a life? Did they suspect the wound was fatal and you were living within a small window of time? Who played God on your behalf that night? A phone call you desired but was not granted—even a prisoner is granted that civil right. An eighteen-year-old young man, you were afraid for me, needing to call your mother one last time, however, someone on that parking lot kept you from your basic right, not extending a courtesy to a dying son lying alone separated from parents, family, love, and comfort. Someone decided your need was not important in that moment.

Who had the gall to keep you "still" and deny your basic rights as a human being to make a phone call? Whose eternal judgment was that in your final moments? I will never have closure on that, baby. It keeps me up at night, it replays over in my mind, robbing me of precious moments. What if I could have had comforting words for you? What if I could have echoed a prayer in your ear as your body went into shock? What if I could have sung softly to you a lullaby to bring you comfort as I have so many times in the still of the night? What if we could have listened to the rhythmic breathing exchanged between mother and son, without words, only hope reverberating between the phones? What if I could have, once again, said the words you were so familiar with "I love you?" I never get tired of saying it, you never get tired of hearing it and reciprocating the response. I'm sure you were met with professional sterility, perhaps being called "buddy" by men in suited armor with no regard for your separation from family. Perhaps, they forgot you were human with the need to hear your mother whisper your name on the other end of the line.

What if? I can't turn the volume down in my head and heart; it screams loudly in the night—every night. What if? What secrets would we have shared; none that has not been stated. You and I shared heartbeats together in synchrony, mine operated in sync with yours. When yours stopped, my heart became dysfunctional—broken heart syndrome. "All the king's horses and all the king's men couldn't put Mama's heart together again." Broken, showing sketchy images in an EKG, a phenomenon requiring lots of cardio evaluation. My heartbeat became irregular, my baby. Why? Because my son's heart no longer beat in cadence with mine. How will mine function without yours? It has lived happily rhythmically for eighteen years, healthy, and unscarred yet now questionable in its stability.

Oh my god! So many pills I am prescribed for a wound only God in his infinite mercy can heal. This heart of mine needs a touch from God, baby boy. Can you ask him to see about your mom? Mercy would be welcomed now. I have been given pills strong enough to knock out a horse, but the noise in my soul can't be quieted. In it is etched the timeline of your death. So here I sit, my son, hushing my soul from the hurt, however, my soul won't be quieted, it needs answers to the aforementioned questions. It needs justice for a murder wrongfully committed. It needs peace, dear boy, that "passeth all understanding." My soul needs solace and refuge, it needs bandages, gauze, and salve for the wound that remains. It needs healing that only God can give. Where is my replacement? There is none. Nothing will fill this void; nothing is designed to.

There will never be another boy, man-child, son, or future father to make me a grandmother. Forty-six minutes in a parking lot with no farewells or love-filled words of encouragement, so I write and pray that these letters reach you. Perhaps, the angels will rush-deliver this one to you because it is quite urgent, and I have been robbed of too much already, my son. I'm expected to sit through a trial and face the heartless murderer who was on a meaningless kill hunt that night. It snatches me back, forcing me to relive the pain all fresh and new like a scab ripped from a wound.

Be still my soul, I whisper to myself. *Just be still.*

It's 4:37 a.m. I will now try to chase the sleep that escapes me every night.

Sweet dreams, my darling.

Eternally yours,
Mom

CHAPTER 2

A LETTER TO CURTIS

SUNDAY, OCTOBER 7, 2018, at 4:20 p.m.
  (Six months prior to death)

CURTIS, YOU ARE TWO MONTHS AND FOUR DAYS AWAY from being recognized by universal laws as an adult, which means that every decision you make at the age of eighteen will be evaluated as the decision of a man versus a boy. The government, the state, your school, and other adults around you will align themselves with your manhood. When you are considered a child, a boy, or young adult, there are leniency laws (set forth by the universe) to protect your innocence. The moment you turn eighteen, those laws are removed.

Therefore—as a parent, as your mother—it is my duty to make sure you are prepared for adulthood in ways you don't know. Life will force you to learn incorrectly or by happenstance, but a parent's sole purpose in life is to protect, provide, and guide. Here is where it gets tricky: it is the child's job to learn. Now that doesn't mean, as parents, we are perfect! There are lessons to be learned from our imperfection as well, like what not to do. We were talking the other night, and you gave me your take on how I handle my finances and what you would do differently. That was good, and it shows that you are making decisions even from our mistakes. Great! Those are the steps that lead you into manhood.

LIFE IS LIKE A BATTLEFIELD FULL OF OPPOSING SIDES:

OPPORTUNITIES VERSUS LACK
    good versus evil
    light versus darkness
    right versus wrong
    excellence versus mediocrity
    discipline versus laziness
    wealth versus poverty

I FEEL THAT IF I DO NOT OFFER YOU MY INSIGHT AND guidance, I fail you as a mother. The choices listed above will be ever-present in your life. Choose wisely. Those choices come cloaked as people and persuasions through things. Choose wisely. These choices will be presented in defined moments of time. Choose wisely.

When you read me your personality type, according to the personality you identified with, you need affirmation from others. The opinion of those around you is paramount in your life. However, here is a secret that you deserve to know: when you value a person's opinion of you, you give them power to control your emotions. You will find your emotions derailing when you perceive that a person's opinion of you is unfavorable. Now listen to me, son, that is literally giving away your power! Also, if your emotions are low, you will create unfavorable opinions of yourself based on *what you think* that person thinks about you! It doesn't even have to be true, it will be what your emotions (in that moment) tell you is true.

Free yourself from the need of approval from others. You have been held hostage to that since you were a child. That mindset breeds *rejection*! You will attract it repeatedly in your life. It's like a blood-sucking leech that will dictate how you perceive life day-to-day. Who's in my corner? Who's got my back? Who's going to be there for me?

You will grow dependent on the emotional value you gain from others. It is a prison to which only you hold the key. It is a way of life in which you are literally controlled by other people's acceptance of you. You have been this way all your life, and as you were reading your personality type to me, you resigned yourself to feel like this is the way it is and nothing can be done about it. But I have good news for you: for every battle you are in, there is proper armor because your opponent doesn't play fair and will always go for the weakest *exposed* point. Think about it, in football, whoever designed the uniform understood that every part that would bring a player to his knees needs to be protected—including the nuts. With that being said, your best armor against *rejection* is *acceptance*.

Remember, I told you that life is like a battlefield with two opposing sides? For you to *overcome* your profound need for acceptance, it must first start with you! You must *accept you* first! You cannot hold *anyone* else to a measure you have created without first meeting that measure yourself! Think about it, would you respect a coach who never played ball? No! Why? Because you know that a coach who played ball knows the play and what it feels like to get knocked around on the field. He has taken a beating on the field and can teach strategy. He has met the *measure* he gives to his team. It's the same with you. You cannot expect *anyone* to love you, accept you, support you, and forgive you better than you. Hmmm…why did I throw in "forgive?" Forgive is what you give for you! It will set you free.

Now what keeps a person from accepting themselves is an aggravating thing usually cloaked by unforgiveness. It's hard to love yourself if you don't forgive yourself, it's hard to fully support yourself without forgiveness. *Forgiveness* on the battlefield of life is the best weapon to kill the spirit of rejection and the need for acceptance from others. Now don't get me wrong, as your mom, I am not saying that we don't need other people, but if you don't get anything else out of this, people will treat you how you treat yourself.

In this life, we teach people how to treat us according to how we *value* ourselves! Do you want loyalty? You know what to do. Be loyal to yourself! Do you want to be loved? You already know. Love yourself! Do you want support? You know where I'm going with this. Support yourself! You want trust? Yes? Therefore, you already know. Trust yourself! Look at yourself in the mirror and tell yourself you are worthy, you are forgiven, you are valuable, you are brilliant, you are kind, you are trustworthy, you are honorable, you are a treasure, you are loyal, you are faithful, you are satisfied, you are grateful, you are handsome, you have winning smile, and whatever else you can throw in there.

I need you and you need to be the best version of yourself because in two months and four days, you will be eighteen. Remember, the universe will catapult you into adulthood. Everything I just shared with you will help you make a *healthy* transition into life as an adult. You are on your way to a happy, whole, and healthy life when you take those keys and free yourself.

Have the super phenomenal day you deserve, son!

Only the best for you,
Mom

CHAPTER 3

AIN'T NO STOPPING US NOW

HEY, my son! I jammed with you all day to the song "Ain't No Stoppin' Us Now" by McFadden and Whitehead. I blared that song during our transition from our home on the east side of town. We had to pack and move to our new home, a new beginning for us. That song to me was very symbolic of where we were at that time in our lives. The lyrics were very much a motivation for the direction we were headed in. The lyrics rang true, and tonight, I dedicate this to you, my son.

AIN'T NO STOPPIN' US NOW!
>We're on the move!
>Ain't no stoppin' us now!
>We've got the groove!
>There's been so many things that's held us down
>But now it looks like things are finally comin' around
>I know we've got a long, long way to go
>And where we'll end up, I don't know

But we won't let nothin' hold us back
We're putting ourselves together
We're polishing up our act!
If you felt we've been held down before
I know you'll refuse to be held down anymore!
Don't you let nothing, nothing
Stand in your way!
I want y'all to listen, listen
To every word I say, every word I say!
Ain't no stoppin' us now!
We're on the move!
Ain't no stoppin' us now!
We've got the groove!
Ain't no stoppin' us now!
We're on the move!
Ain't no stoppin' us now!
We've got the groove!
I know you know someone that has a negative vow
And if you're trying to make it, they only push you aside
They really don't have nowhere to go
Ask them where they're going, they don't know
But we won't let nothin' hold us back
We're gonna put ourselves together
We're gonna polish up our act!
And if you've ever been held down before
I know you'll refuse to be held down anymore!
Don't you let nothing, nothing
Stand in your way!
I want y'all to listen, listen
To every word I say, every word I say!

Ain't no stoppin' us now!
We're on the move!
Ain't no stoppin' us now!
We've got the groove!
Ain't no stoppin' us now!
We're on the move!
Ain't no stoppin' us now!
We've got the groove!

. . .

I LOVE YOU! VISIT YOUR SISTER, SHE NEEDS encouragement! I will carry you in my heart as I sleep tonight, baby, because I especially missed you today. I sent this song to all your friends to enjoy.

Eternally,
Mom

CHAPTER 4

ANOTHER SUN, SON

THE BEAMS of light flicker in my window, bringing with it the constant awareness that you are not here. I awoke this morning with a flood of memories of you, chasing each one down, taking a long, keen look, holding on to the memories—each and everyone that I could find.

When I let you go through the family scrapbook of the last seventeen years of photos with one of your friends, in the back of my mind, I felt it was important to you to share with him your life (as though you knew time would be short for you). I remember having a fleeting thought of all the reasons why I wanted so many photos so I could remember you and your sister. I knew you didn't understand the value of time and memories. Now that book is gone. I have nothing but the etched places in my mind of you at various intervals of your life. In that invaluable scrapbook were the various stages of all our lives. I pray that somehow it surfaces. I truly believe you removed it from the house. Maybe it is in the trunk of the car or, perhaps, your friend moved it. Maybe it is in the garage somewhere (let's hope), although it still hasn't surfaced.

All the years of lovingly gathered images and captured moments and times are gone. Ask the angels to help me out on this one and miraculously cause that book to surface, please. It ties the future to the past. I need it.

I LOVE YA, LITTLE MONKEY. I NEED THIS FAVOR, ASK GOD NICELY for me.

I will be forever grateful.

Hugs and kisses,
Mom

PS: ANGELS, RUSH DELIVERY, AND WHILE YOU'RE AT IT, can one of you help me find my children's scrapbook? Thanks!

CHAPTER 5

FROM MOM WITH LOVE

HEY, my baby! Yes, I said it, my baby! I told you, you will always be my baby (even though your physical body is gone, the "spirit you" is eternal). You got to love that, right?

Anyway, sorry I didn't write you, I have been pouting with God. Let him know he's still sovereign, he is still amazing (he gave me you), and he's still my rock. Tell him I haven't forgotten who he is. I'm just bruised. I wanted more time with you.

By the way, give my love to all our family. Kiss your uncle Judah for me. Tell Mrs. Melinda Walker I said hello. That will blow her mind...she'll blink, then laugh and tell you, "Yeah, that's your momma."

So I'm not sure where to start, so much has happened since the memorial. A network of adults and students will be working with me on your LLC community tournament; it will be huge and impactful for the community overall. You left an unbelievable legacy, little guy. You changed an entire county! Also, I had to put our guest out. I know you are not surprised. I have done all I can do, and it's time he grows up.

By the way, Destiny has a dog; we named him Ranger. He doesn't bark; he's a one-year-old mixed Rottweiler and Boxer (cute as a button). I got the dog to help Dee cope with her grief. It seems to be a good fit for her, but he needs to be trained. Anyway, the guys think he (Ranger) reminds them of you; they come by to check on me sometimes. They loved you dearly, son; you made a difference in their lives. I love that about you.

(long pause)

Little boy, forgive the delay. I got distracted with tears, and then the plumbers came by to fix the sink, and I had to go see about the dog.

All right, as I was saying earlier, things have happened. On May 29, your first scholarship in your name (Long Live Curt Track & Field Scholarship) was presented at the annual FPCHS track-and-field awards banquet. How cool was that? Your dear friend was the recipient. Also, I was presented with your honorary diploma! Son, you graduated! The superintendent presented me with your diploma. I walked across the stage for you, son! God allowed you to graduate. It was what you were looking forward to doing…well, you did it! It aired on television on channel 2 news! Yay! And you will be giving out scholarships in your name every year! You accomplished what was dear to your heart! The scholarship has your name on it. Isn't that awesome? You wanted to go to college and run track, and now you will help many kids do that every single year! Also, your track team ran for you, and a good friend of mine ran in a relay in New York in the pouring rain for you, wearing your LLC Long Live T-shirt. By the way, one of your friends won a championship in your name, and another took you to the prom via proxy. The kids are finding all kinds of ways to honor your legacy.

The FPCHS film department made a documentary about you; a sports film company out of Jacksonville came to the house yesterday to film a documentary in honor of your life and legacy. Special appearances were made by by, your Auntie Candace your close friends and coaches giving the viewing audience a glance of your character and life on and off the field. The documentary was moving and when the cameras stopped rolling, the tears began to flow. It was a moment that drew each participant a little closer to each other as each shared a memory of you.

Okay, that's what I have for now because I'm tired of writing.

I LOVE YOU. I HOPE YOU GET TEXT MESSAGES IN HEAVEN. I feel like you should. I'm going to ask God nicely if you can receive this. If you do, remember to tell him "Mom says thank you."

Okay, love ya.
Mom

PS: FROM MY HEART TO HEAVEN, PLEASE GIVE THIS TO MY baby. Pretty please with a cherry on top?

CHAPTER 6

BROKEN BUT BETTER

LITTLE GUY, I firmly believe that some things that are broken are not meant to be put back together to mimic their original design. Broken things in the hands of a masterful designer become couture, one-of-a-kind pieces. I must accept this as I am learning to accept the shards of my life that remain, now glued back together by divine destiny and purpose. I have no idea where this journey will lead me, all my comfort has been disrupted, dismantled, and discarded. Lost is what I am, weary of trying to be found, unloved and weary of desiring love. Who is the shell of a woman that is left behind? One whose life has been altered by unimaginable pain, and yet somewhere in my broken pieces, hope is an element that helps bind the smallest fragments together. I am learning to accept that what is done is done and will not have permission to ever repeat itself in my life. Whatever lesson that should have been gleaned from the travesty of losing you, I will embrace it so I never have to experience this journey again.

Forgiveness is the design element that causes the new vessel to take shape and gain unprecedented value far above who I was before. The potter chose this element to add a signature look, style, and essence—adding a beauty and radiance that did not exist before— making me exquisite, noticeable, desirable, and worthy of display in the museum of life among other priceless artifacts. Broken but better, bringing value to others through my pain and experiences. I was entrusted to love and care for the most precious baby boy sent to me with beautiful thick hair, deep dimples, and giggles that never quit until they were replaced with the deep, warm vibrato of a man whose mirth was contagious and healing to many.

Broken but better, son, because I had to forgive the very one who lent you to me. He knew I was angry and confused and hurt beyond measure, but I had to release and forgive the very one who gives me my next breath. I had to do the same for the father who helped procreate life with me (producing you), and I also had to forgive myself. I am still working on that, but the awareness of its importance is the road map to the destination of the next phase of my life. A beacon and guide, if you will, to help me stay the course and not be tripped by hurtful memories or would've-could've-should've moments. They haven't magically disappeared, they resurface at the most inopportune time, supplied by emotional triggers from sights, smells, sounds, familiarity, geography, people, places, ideologies, dreams, and the ghosts of the past. The fact that I am aware of this makes me better, but I have not fully arrived, however, sheer determination to get to the other side of "through" is the force I utilize for a better tomorrow.

Broken but better, knowing that your transition home has you in a far better place than the life you knew that yields unprecedented pains, upsets, and unexpected events. You are far above the pain and turmoil you left behind. I imagine you at your optimal self, enjoying eternity and in awe of absolutely everything and in eager anticipation of the reunion of our family together again. I have been blessed to have a large capacity of love, and that makes me better because I have still been able to love without restraint despite my personal losses. It's one of the most important design features masterfully crafted into my new design.

Don't you worry about me, baby, mom's making strides. I'm determined to leave the identity of brokenness behind and only align with just being better.

Loving you with everything I got, boy,
Mom

CHAPTER 7

CHECKING IN ON YA

GOOD MORNING, son. I wish, somehow, you could bend God's ear to see about your little cousin, Izear. He is in that emotional space you were in when your uncle Judah died. I think I'm going to pick him up and have him spend a week with me. He needs to know you were okay. Maybe I will have your friends surround him so he can know that you were loved, and your death was not in vain. Maybe he needs to hear the testimonials from the kids here of how you made positive impacts in their lives. Izear does not like to hear the mention of your name, he covers his ears to keep the pain of your death associated with your name minimized.

Your assailant never considered the ramifications of the profound pain your loss would bring. You had little cousins you spent time mentoring, Dallin, Deuce, Ariana, Izear, Ayanah, and distant cousins. Unfortunately, these children will have a deeply embedded wound because of the evil intention of a young man who calculated a senseless murder to make a name for himself. He did not know how his actions would negatively impact the youth in the neighborhood who participated in the young readers book club you worked with for four years nor the little league teams you helped coach. Then there are the little siblings of your friends and all the younger students who aspired "to be like Curt."

I would hate to be the defense attorney, fighting for the rights of a heartless murderer. It makes me wonder how one sleeps at night when representing someone without remorse. The job, or rather the goal, of the defense attorney is to gain a lesser sentence for their client even if it means character assassination of the victim, willfully selling their souls to a demoralized conscienceless state to redeem heartless murderers, which means they themselves are no better than the murderer. I pray that God will provide justice in your case, son, and heal the brokenhearted.

On a different note, I want you to know about your sister; she has taken a very active role in her recovery through exercise. It reminds me of how you overcame your own struggles during the breakup of our family. Remember how you pulled yourself up? I was talking to one of the mothers at a friend's baby's shower, and she was saying how it was an inspiration to her and others who knew your story to watch you transition. You and Destiny were the recipients of the same shameful darkness unleashed by your dad, and you both have made remarkable strides despite it. Destiny excelled in school, throwing all her focus on her academics instead of the scar he left in her heart. You excelled in sports despite the loss and remorse of his absence. You both decided not to be victims of a failed support system from your dad, and both of you made a conscious decision to heal. Destiny's pain, however, was extended because she not only lost her wayward dad, but she also lost her brother—two solid male figures in her life. Just like you, she was bent, but she didn't break.

I observed Destiny today; she is amazing, graceful, and poised even under the weight of your absence. She has chosen to honor your memory by purchasing a skateboard and learning to ride it. She wakes up early each morning, pounding the pavement, running out the hurt in her heart and stretching past her anguish through yoga to heal psychologically and physically. One thing I feel confident in: Destiny will emerge from this, covered by the prayers of friends, family, strangers including attorneys, deputies, doctors, civil workers, city officials and the commissioner, city councilmen, school board members, teachers and students, seniors, children, postal workers, grocery clerks, and others we don't know. So many people are praying for us but especially for her. God is faithful. He has people covering us near and far in cities across the nation. I pray that the prayers don't stop.

Anyway, I'm picking this back up from earlier this morning (sorry for the delay). I experienced both a high and a low today. You would be proud of me. I finally registered for swimming lessons at the Belle Terre Swim & Raquet Club. Yay me! I decided to do whatever is necessary to help me cope with your loss. It's crucial that I work this stress out of my body, and I figured what better way to do that than swim, right? It's a win-win from the aspect of overcoming my fear of water and learning how to survive in water. I am doing things in this time of my life that I have never done before, and that is refreshing. That was indeed my high moment for the day! Unfortunately, I also experienced a low that completely blindsided me. The proof for the artwork on your headstone came back today, and it made me weep because of the finality of your loss. I saw the embossed letters of your name and your span of life: December 11, 2000–April 13, 2019. What a crude reality to see your etched face on the front of the headstone, it was surreal, I wept. My friend, Linda, texted me for me to know that April 13 marked the beginning of a new life for you. It comforted me a little.

With love,
Mom

CHAPTER 8

CHERISHING MEMORIES

HEY, kiddo, you already know I'm up at zero dark thirty. You are always mindful to rendezvous with your mom around this time, you know I will rise and reach for you. You are here to listen, reassure, and soak up my presence; you are here to just be my son, a shoulder to lean on, and lend me your undivided attention. I have been waiting for a sign, often feeling slighted, because your friends would tell me you come to them when they are at their lowest moments. I would think, *Why don't you come to me, baby?* But I see now that you do.

Each time I awake with an urgency to write, penning words to paper or typing out my heart on a device, I now know that it is you who waits for me. I am awakened out of a deep sleep, sharply alert with a sense of longing for my only son. It's not a slow, languid rolling out of sleep, it is an acute awareness that causes sleep to give way to my need to hear you and be heard. It is in these moments that I have vivid recollections of precious moments: your facial expressions, the furrowed crease in your brows if you were perplexed, your sensitivity to others, your keen but very mature and artful manner of listening and hearing, your analytical approach to absolutely everything—you were not an abstract person but one with eagle eye observation—and your penetrating writing skills as a lyricist, consciously poetic.

Simply exemplified, nothing escaped you. You profoundly wrote out your heart's secrets, sometimes to music and often—metaphorically, at times—to a cadence. You would read some of your writings to me, and I would look at you with wonder as I often did, thinking, *Where did you come from?* It was as if you had lived well beyond your years; you had a sense and sensibility that was akin to that of a mature man who had lived decades before well submersed in the nuances of this thing we called life. When you shared with me your penned thoughts, I was often stunned at the amazing gift you kept well hidden from your teachers. I was in awe of the insight that you expressed so freely, coming from a deep and penetrating place where you often unveiled your observations, frustrations, and expectations through a rhythm and rhyme. Writing was a gift passed down to you from your grandparents. All my siblings are talented writers, lyricists, and artists. Therefore, you inherently obtained that talent, however, I will admit, it far surpasses my skill set.

In the wee hours of the morning, I have vivid recollections of your pensive, no-nonsense approach to just about everything. You were especially sensitive about so many things, and your perception of most things was often shaped by your deep sense of reflection. Your feelings were easily hurt because you loved without bias and cared without limits. You were loyal to your friends, and your capacity to care was beyond the measure of most youth. You met everyone—no one was exempted—old, young, male, female, Black, White, Hispanic, disabled, castaways, rich, poor, affluent, extrovert, introvert, gay, straight, awkward, or popular. You often extended out a hand and entered a relationship with eye-to-eye contact and a firm shake after a pointed introduction.

When you were six, I made you practice introducing yourself, telling you to make strong eye contact, cautioning you that the first person who looked away loses. You enjoyed this as if it were a game, the challenge to not be the first to look away. You could not engage in this simple exercise without a wide sloppy grin and silly smile. I would taunt you in a sing-songy voice, "Cuuurtis, you looked away first." You would giggle and beg me to do it again, determined to keep eye contact. I made you practice announcing your name; you did it with gusto, revealing nothing but dimples. This became your signature entry into many people's lives: a firm handshake, eye-to-eye contact, and a bold announcement of your name. No one was exempted.

You were a child who loved to please. I saw that as a potential threat. Until you reached sixth grade, it was quite a challenge to break you out of that profound need to please; but truthfully, you always put the needs of others first. I felt it would be an easy segue into a life of following rather than that of leadership. I felt it was necessary to balance that part of your personality with a strong sense of leadership. I talked to you often about not allowing yourself to be "influenced" but become the one to influence and impact the lives of others. I often shared with you that no one with limited life experiences should be your moral compass, that you should surround yourself with men you esteemed and learn from them. I told you that no one outside our doors should have the greater influence over your life than your mother, reminding you no one would ever love you more and have the best intentions for your life. After all, I had the stretch marks that required your loyalty, respect, and priority.

In our home, I had rules that seemed strict, but you needed the boundaries. You tried to push against them at times, but you were raised from a little child to be respectful, and indeed, you were. It was a stellar quality I was proud of, my hard work paid off even though you often complained I was the strictest mom in Palm Coast (LOL). I used to tell you that you bore my name, and you had to wear it well. I would often say to you as you left the house, "Curtis, nothing negative about you had better come back to me when you walk out that door." You would say in an over exasperated tone, "I know, Mom."

When you and Destiny were little, I would take you guys to the store or we would be in the house, and you both would be up to some mischievous activity. I would hear you in an awestruck voice exclaim to your sister, "Destiny, Mom really does have eyes in the back of her head, how does she know?" Often, I would have to go in my room or walk away and just chuckle. Your dad traveled all the time, and more times than not, it was just the three of us, intertwined into one another's lives. When your dad came home, you craved his presence, and he would spend quality time with you: fishing, hunting, and teaching you how to mow the lawn or tinker outside. As a family, we went camping and traveled quite a bit. You had a good life, son, up until your junior year, but by then, you knew enough to know how to survive on your own. You had a keen sense of finances and a strong set of disciplines, contributed by key authority figures in your life like your coaches, your cousins, uncle and grandfather, and strong men in the community who made awesome contributions to your life, granting you mentorship and structure as needed.

I woke up this morning and wanted to recall certain memories of you. I heard from Donovan from the W section yesterday; he talked about how you were a "light" in his life, describing you as pure. That tells me that all the disciplines paid off, and your father and I raised a son whose legacy will live on, as Donovan said, through the lives of others.

I can no longer touch you or cup my hands around your chin or kiss you tenderly as only a mother can. I can no longer chide you about driving in my car, smelling like a jock (you and as many sweaty boys who could fit in my car). I made you place blankets on the seats, OMG, it didn't help! I can no longer put ice on your chest to wake you up in the morning, angry as a bear; I can no longer hear you singing at the top of your lungs in *my* shower! You always insisted on using *my* shower, and I always threatened you, but you hated the way Destiny kept you guys' bathroom with haircare products, makeup, and whatever teenage girls obsess over. You would come to me and say, "Mom, talk to your daughter." I can no longer try to offer you comfort when your eczema would flare up under extreme stress, you hated it.

When you died, it was the first thing I thought about: no more suffering from that. You described the flare-up as torment even with the medication. I can no longer run my hands *across* your hair because it was too thick for me to weave my fingers *through* it. I can no longer smell the waft of your father's Burberry cologne you wore going out the door as you would leave the house. Your dad mildly complained about you not replacing it (LOL). You were obsessed with smelling good and looking good. Your things were neatly kept, you were particular about how you represented yourself.

I can no longer threaten you about making sure the dishes were prewashed before going into the dishwasher, you absolutely hated that with a passion. One day, you muttered "do it yourself." Before I knew it, I lifted you off the ground with my hand under your chin. The shock and awe stretched your eyes so wide. You were fifteen years old and taller than me; I picked you up from pure adrenaline! You cried that day, it scared you, but we never discussed the dishes and how *I preferred* them cleaned again. It made your dad nervous; he had never seen me exude such strength. I told him, "Never underestimate the power of a mother, we can lift cars with one hand if we have to rescue our child or knock them clear into tomorrow." I'm smiling as I recall that moment. I think your dad gained a new respect for me that day (LOL). I taught respect early so I would never have to fear you later when you became strong enough and capable of exerting your strength against me or anyone else in authority. Faith was the moral compass in our house, and you embraced it and lived it until you took your last breath.

Missing you is the echo of each heartbeat, a rhythm to which I will never grow accustomed. The unyielding ache cannot be replaced, so instead, I write, knowing that my small request to have these letters reach you anchors my sanity. I love you, mama's boy. Your twentieth birthday is coming up, and this week has been an emotional roller coaster, bittersweet even. I need to capture moments in my recollecting and place them safely away. When my eyes grow dim, maybe, perhaps, one of Destiny's children will read to me the stories that I have captured, the legacy of their uncle Curtis "Curt" Israel Gray.

Loving you completely without limits,

Mom

Chapter 9

To Medicate or Not to Medicate?
That Is the Question

Browsing through my phone, I found this text I sent to you after your therapy session with Dr. Whatshername. She recommended medication for you. I was very hesitant about you being on medication because of the side effects they tell you on TV that it "may increase thoughts of suicide." How ironic was this post, as now I am medicated to deal with your death. I think this was a text for you in September 2018:

You are a big, strong man. You are not that fragmented, scared boy you were just a few months ago. Take a closer look at this picture: confident and comfortable.

You do not *ever need a substance* to dictate your ability to manage your emotions, you only need strong discipline and guidance to help you overcome the low moments you experience now and those that will come as you continue in your journey as a man.

You have been labeled as having "depression," but depression is circumstance-driven! It sounds enormous, but it is a condition of the mind that can be controlled with *cognitive therapy*, which means you need coping skills that will navigate you through life's difficult moments. There will be plenty. As an adult, you will learn the art of survival. You will learn not to be manipulated by people because people come and go out of your life. You will learn to love yourself better than anyone else, which is the biggest weapon against depression, and you will learn to liberate yourself from secrets. To "de-press" something means to hold it in under immense pressure. Never give another soul that much power over you.

Curtis, you harness the power over depression through self-love and acceptance, along with confidence and the ability to overcome life's challenges. Listen, son, you can't do it alone. You need a life coach (counselor), but you need to show up and be in the moment for your own self-healing. Stop avoiding the truth, the truth of who you are and where you are in this moment. When you know the truth of who you are, you can deal with your weaknesses like a man. A weakness in your life only reveals an *opportunity* for something to be evaluated and strengthened or eliminated if it is harmful to your overall good.

My life coaches are the motivational speakers I listen to daily. Son, if I don't teach you anything else, just know that every battle you have in life starts in the mind! Whether it's through chemical imbalance, trauma, mental disorder, low self-esteem, or just life. *It all starts in the mind.*

When you can counter the negative challenges of the mind (the words, the images, and the constant negative chatter that wakes you up in the morning and goes on in your head as you sleep and wakes you up like a constant drip), then you win! How can you overcome that? Two things:

1. You can control a thought with words spoken out loud. When a negative thought is bouncing around in your head, you must state out loud (with words) the opposing results you want to manifest. Words like: I'm an overcomer, no weapon formed against me shall prosper, God in me is more than enough, I have untapped potential, I win, I do not lose or fail. Or how about this one: nope, I will not accept that!

2. You can place every thought with a new image. Reimagine the outcome under positive terms. Only you can control this. The mind is powerful. I go back into my negative thoughts and even dreams and repaint the picture. I tell my head how things will turn out; I will not accept anything unless I approve it! This is how the super successful people in our society become successful, they imagine it first!

I DON'T WANT YOU ON A MIND-BENDING DRUG. HOWEVER, a low-dosage anxiety pill may be beneficial. I am going to request cognitive therapy for you. I love you, and we *will deal* with the other stuff tonight.

I VIVIDLY RECALL THE CONVERSATION WE HAD THE following morning after I sent you that text. Now I'm in a quandary because I find myself resisting the very advice I gave you. My, how things have changed, and I can't physically handle life without the medication I was prescribed to cope with the horrific survival of your death. Until a person experiences travesty in the way you, Destiny, and I have, one can only imagine.

With love,
Mom
XOXOXO

CHAPTER 10

DANCE, BABY, DANCE

"EVERY TIME I DANCE, I turn into a better version of me." I saw this quote in this video on the power of healing through dance. How dancing releases "frozen images" from muscles and tissues. I immediately thought about you and how you were able to pull yourself out of depression by dancing. I watched the videos your friends made of you. You danced every chance you got with your friends. Without knowing it, you used dance therapy to free yourself and those around you. Studies show that dancing is more effective than seeing a psychiatrist or doing standard exercise. Wow! You danced all the time, every day, often making me and your friends participate. Dancing and singing were your superpowers! You healed yourself through dance without even realizing it. I watched you come out of a dark black hole of grief and depression. It was like watching you gaining a new lease on life, a surge of genesis. Dance was your coping mechanism; without knowing it, you developed a unique path to self-discovery in a short period of time. Excellent, son!

With your foundation, dance therapy, art therapy, and color therapy will be used to help youth and others heal past trauma. I'm going to have a video compilation of all your Snapchat stories and videos, bouncing around all over Palm Coast. When I do the presentation for the foundation, I will show this video compilation to the attendees so they can see this as a viable solution in trauma therapy. Hey, babe, I'm excited!

Anyway, this won't be a long text, I have got to take Destiny shopping this morning.

By the way, your friends are getting cool tats in your honor. A few got the same exact tat (Psalms 23:6) as you with #LLC on it. The kids are really trying to work through their grief. You will never be forgotten, sweetheart; your legacy is bigger than what we know now because it keeps growing. Remember, I told you your life would have national and international impact! You wait and see. Of course, I will always send you a text, baby, and keep you abreast of what is happening. Your story will liberate thousands upon thousands over many generations to come. Your legacy lives on, pumpkin.

Love you, my dancing boy,
Mom

PS: Angels, get this to my baby.

CHAPTER 11

HI, BABY GUY!

EARTH HAS no sorrow that heaven cannot heal. I love you, my baby. Please tell all our family hi for me. I spoke to D's mom; she said Dee wants closure. There is a lot of speculation about what happened that night. All your friends feel that you took a bullet for someone else. I believe that is true.

I just finished watching a documentary about clean water. It was intriguing to say the least; during this man's story, Mr. Scott Harrison, the founder of Charity Water, there was a story about a little nine-year-old girl who raised $220 on her birthday to give to children without clean water. She didn't raise the amount she wanted, so her mother told her to try again next year. That little girl, Rachel Beckwith, did not get a chance to "try again next year" because she was killed in a fatal car accident. The story was covered by the news, and suddenly, people began to talk about the legacy she left behind with the $220 dollars she raised on her birthday. Her original goal was three hundred dollars, but sadly, she was killed and would not have that opportunity. Americans started donating nine dollars in her name until over $1,200,000 was raised, and the organization, Charity Water, flew her family over to Africa to see the impact their daughter made in the lives of the nation she sponsored.

My point is that I believe God allows people to exit tragically

in ways that stir the hearts of others especially when the work they started is too great, and he measures their hearts against a cause and knows that in the exit of their physical life, their hearts' desire to effect change would be best served in their departure. That little girl, Rachel's name, will live on forever because her heart was in the right place. I believe that when you want to do something that is so huge as a gift to humanity and God knows you will be limited in your effort, he may call you home in a way that grabs people's attention so that he can work through you still but get glory from your life as well as death.

I needed to see this documentary. It helped me to understand why you had to go like you did. Your fatal exit has put things in motion that through the goodness and large capacity of your heart to help others, God will use your name to help others impacted by trauma. Can I tell you something, son? I have no idea what I am doing with your foundation, I just believe now that the pain of your departure has something amazing attached to it. There were some things that you really wanted to do and tried to accomplish on your own, including both positive mental health and financial literacy for youth. With this foundation, those things you desired are possible, and now you will be able to see the magnitude of your desire to serve others, reflected in those you leave behind.

You said, "Mom, promise me you will be great." You knew you were leaving me. Listen, son, I will, by God's help and strength, be great. I live by this creed daily. As a matter of fact, it is the cultural fiber of your foundation. We will be great! We will make a difference! We will serve the kids you loved even as you lay dying, you loved them to death! We will help their families with this mental health crisis that has impacted our society. We will care in the same way you did. We will add on the financial literacy you were so passionate about. We will partner with other organizations to be impactful. Your exit is the force that will ensure my promise to be great. I now vow this to God himself that I will live greatly for him.

Please tell him thank you for helping me to understand. I didn't before, and I was angry. But you are not gone, nor you are forgotten, just multiplied and spread out to serve others at a greater capacity. The Bible tells us it's better to have a good name, and, sweetheart, God covered your name. Curtis Israel Gray means "courteous prince among men, both Black and White."

I PROMISE, SON, I WILL BE *GREAT*!

With love,
Mom

PS: ANGELS, RUSH DELIVERY, PLEASE.

CHAPTER 12

FROM MOM TO MAN

HEY, li'l dude, have you met your family yet? Your grandparents, aunties, uncles, and cousins? Give them all my love.

I had company all this week, and it threw me off my regimen a bit. I have been working tirelessly on the foundation, getting all the legalities taken care of. I have had several interviews; everyone is waiting for it to be released. I'm going to continue the work you started, making sure the kids here in Palm Coast have effective resources to get the help they need for any crisis they may be experiencing. I also want to incorporate the stock market group you started. One of your friends received a sizable tuition gift (10,000 dollars). He announced that since you taught him how to purchase and sell stocks, he is going to invest his money in the stock market. How cool is that? That was all you, baby! Your friends and the people you mentored are finding ways to honor the positive impact you made in their lives.

As a matter of fact, a documentary was made, in your honor, of different peers you helped or encouraged. I watched it several times; it made me cry. You gave support and nurture to the youth around here, and many of them are in a tailspin with their pain. Your peer group still reaches out to me to make sure I'm good; you really made a difference, baby, and were a great influence. Coach Chris has been mentoring the kids and reminding them that you were a great example to follow. He said that is the legacy you left behind. By the way, he is now my and Destiny's personal trainer to help us work the stress of your tragic loss out of our bodies. He will be by today to help us with some much-needed all-over body workouts.

I hope you are watching over your sister; she is battling depression. I'm going to get her to a counselor really soon, she needs guidance. The county seems to be at a loss for how to handle a crisis of this proportion. When I get your foundation up and running, this is one way I can give back in your name—by helping our community heal from this senseless violence. I am rallying the community for a back-to-school "stand against violence" tournament. The kids so desperately want to actively find ways to stand together.

I am finding out more about what happened that night. It seems that Marion had been on social media, bragging about how he killed or "smoked" the young man who was run over by a sanitation truck while working. Apparently, the kids on Snapchat were calling him out, saying he didn't "smoke" anybody. Sadly, Marion felt he had a point to prove. On the night of the shooting, you exited the smoke shop and were called to the vehicle in which Marion, the shooter, waited for you. The instigator, a female named Alex, incited Marion using gang terms like "looks like you want some smoke." At that point, without hesitation, Marion pulled the trigger that released a fatal blow—a kill shot to the abdomen.

I pray for justice. It was senseless, and neither one of them have any remorse. I feel if Palm Coast doesn't make an example of him, you will be the first of others who will suffer as a result of a broken system. I'm sharing this with you, it is bad, I know, and it is a lot to forgive, but I am asking God to help me forgive it. It will take time and a willful decision, but with God, all things are possible. There are so many things and people to forgive in this situation. I have watched you forgive hard things that even some adults would struggle with. Many nights, we talked about forgiveness and how it is not for the recipient but to free one's own soul. That is where I am now.

I know as you laid there dying, not understanding how you could be shot by someone without a cause—no argument, no history, no fight, no hostility—plus the lack of urgency to get you to the hospital and my absence, you also had a lot to forgive. I know you did it though because the sergeant who arrived in the scene first said you were in absolute peace. I feel certain that may explain why the paramedics didn't make haste to get you to Halifax. I don't know… but now I too have all these things to forgive and release, and it is not easy. I watched that boy, Marion, and the girl, Alex, sit through the arraignment without a care; I must find it in my heart to forgive that. Only God can help me.

I love you, son. You overcame a lot. I'm proud to be your mother. Your dad told me the night of your death that the three of you (you, him, and your friend) met for dinner, and the two of you reconciled, and you told him you were not afraid to die. He knew that you had made peace in your heart with God. Let me tell you, baby, that is the only thing that gives me any peace in this senseless death, that you made peace in your heart with God and with your dad. I know I will see you again in heaven. God allowed your body to depart this earth, but he saved your soul for an eternity with him.

When I watched the documentary of your peers, talking about the positive impact you made in their lives, my heart wept with pain and pride. You made me proud. The mark of excellent character is not what is done when people are watching but the quality of life you live when people are not. That boy, Marion, was out, looking for a kill that night. You were out, trying to provide a place for your friend to lay his head. Your death was not in vain. You died doing what you did when you were living: helping others. On that night, one boy became a murderer and the other a martyr. One boy's mother must hang her head in shame, and the other boy's mother is carrying the torch her son left behind to continue to help others. I miss you dearly, but you are with me daily. Every time God blesses me to be a blessing to a family, the community, and the kids and friends you left behind, I do it in your honor, son.

#LLC—long live Curt (and you will in the hearts of every life you have touched).

I'm writing this to give us both some closure, my baby; I know you laid there in complete bewilderment as to why a stranger would shoot you, not understanding *why*. The media wanted to say it was because of an altercation, a fight. It was no such thing; the kids said you never even had a chance to speak. They said you were smiling when you got shot. Unbelievable! I have wept and wept; it *is a lot* to forgive!

You can finally rest in peace, son. Now we wait for justice.

With love,
Mom

CHAPTER 13

FROM MOM TO CURTIS WITH LOVE

HEY, baby guy, I'm missing you really fiercely! My soul is vexed with the details around your departure. The attack against you was very strategic; it took place while I was out of my territory. What a nasty underhanded move! I'm angry, and there is nothing I can do about it except trust that our father God had and does have a master plan. If he doesn't, I'm at a loss for words, therefore, I must believe that in this very thing, I must have faith that he is still sovereign and that he reigns.

The one thing I am most confident in without wavering even slightly is that you are indeed with the Lord. In this, my faith is anchored only because since I was a child, I learned that remission of sins and the Holy Ghost are a gift promised for our children and all who are far off and as many as the Lord shall call (Acts 2:38). Therefore, while the strategy was sneaky, you remain the *victor* and were made more than a conqueror. You believed, and it was counted to you for righteousness.

About those you left behind…Curtis, so many of these kids can look to the example you left. It was a seed planted that will produce much fruit. You lived a transparent life; even if you messed up, you were man enough to expose it. Many men do not have that trait of honor. You were always witnessed by your peers as someone whose trying to do better, making wise choices, and working through your pain and conflict. You did all those things openly. You found a way to bare your soul so others could follow the example you left behind; that there is hope in adversity if you are pushing forward to healing. You did it, baby! You did it! You became the example I admonished you to become. You listened, and you executed! I am a proud mother of the man you became, Curtis Israel Gray!

Today and every day, I choose to celebrate every victory you left behind—from your athletic accomplishments to your silent prayers for guidance for your life. I choose to celebrate that you lived your life out loud and on purpose, with dedication to help others. You served others from those in authority to your peers. You served, and you did well. I celebrate the smile that was your gift. No one else could smile like you. It was infectious and healing, and it brought joy and comfort to many. Something so simple and beautiful was your weapon, your armor, and your shield against the darkness that surrounded you when your world came crashing down. You found your smile again, and you began to dance everywhere, allowing others to join in your celebration of rebirth and purpose. You were and are my champion, and I am humbled to be called your mother.

I was chosen to bear the pleasure and the grief of your life and your death. Honestly, if I could do it all over again, I would for, indeed, you are my priceless treasure. Although your body is not here, I still get joy kissing your photos, speaking softly so you can hear. I miss you, and the weight of that has anguish that cannot be described. Son, I would choose to have you again, carry you again for nine months, but I would beg for an extension or an exchange of life. I would. I don't think this is fair, but we all have our crosses to bear, and this unthinkable pain happens to be mine.

I thoroughly enjoyed you—even our crazy spats. You taught me how to listen. It will benefit any man that comes into my life (smile). You taught me how to be inclusive and less judgmental. You taught me that life matters and how we live it should be lived to the fullest. You taught me how to dance and dance and dance through pain and hardship. You taught me how to relax and chill. I love that because I still struggle with it. You taught me what a *real man* looks like. You were indeed that. I did good. I did an amazing job. When you were eight years old, you would not let me do any heavy lifting. Your dad was always MIA, but he taught you how to do a man's job. He did good as well. Between the two of us, you possessed that best quality each of us offered. You are amazing still. I celebrate those traits because they are priceless. Now I can say, "To God be the glory."

Now listen, my baby guy, don't you fret for me. I will see you when God calls me home. I made him a promise, and I aim to keep it. I promised him I would serve him all the days of my life, and even in this life of extreme pain, I have upheld my end of the bargain. He promised me that this promise would be for my children as well so one day we will see one another again. In the meantime, I have work to do. I submitted the paperwork for your foundation. It will touch lives here and spread across the nation. It won't take long for it to ignite. Remember, you passed the torch, and now, as you would say, "It's about to be lit!"

Well, my son, until next time, love, hugs, and kisses from your mom! Like lots of love, an abundance of hugs, and endless kisses. I treasure all the extra love I gave you while you breathed.

Therefore, I have no regrets. I did not withhold love; I gave it all and then some to last you many lifetimes. In that regard, I am confident, and I did so with *great capacity*. I poured out my love to you like an inexhaustible container that never runs empty. I'm still doing it. Neither dimensions and time nor eternity can expire my love for you, son. It's my gift, one I passed on to you. Your capacity for love was also expandable, and I feel your love for your mom all the way from heaven's gates. Thank you, I know you wonder if I can feel you. I can. It's only your body that's absent, and now you can experience the love of a loving Father up close and personal. You will then know why I raised you like I did. I'm sure you got to heaven and thought, *Mom was right.*

Hey, by the way, do they let you keep your haircut in heaven? Just curious…one to ponder. I know that look and grin on your face right now as you shake your head with a big grin, asking, "What?" Yep, only I would ask about your haircut. Just saying.

Much love,
Mom

CHAPTER 14

GONE ONE YEAR

I RECEIVED the news of your departure in a bathroom stall at the QuikTrip after 3:00 a.m. It's now 3:13 a.m. I am reliving the details of that dreadful night. A frantic Destiny called me approximately around 2:20 a.m., "Mom, something is wrong with Curtis. My friends are calling me, saying, 'Destiny, I'm sorry about your brother.' It's all over Instagram." My heart knew, but I needed facts.

I called Flagler sheriff's department and was put on hold. I called again and was made to wait. "Ma'am, we will call you back when we hear something." No mother should ever have to "wait." I called back. "Ma'am, even if we knew something, we couldn't give that kind of information out over the phone."

I called your friend, he would not answer. I called again, no answer. Why wouldn't he answer? My stomach knew, my heart knew! I called Ms. Nicole and asked her to get to the hospital right away. She wasn't immediate family, so they wouldn't release information to her. Your auntie Candace and uncle Ank weren't granted privileged information because they were not your mother or father. I called your dad for the third time, half screaming, "What is taking you so long to get there! He's been shot!"

Destiny called and asked me in the tiniest little voice, "Mommy, please get there safe." She was taking an emergency flight to Florida from Atlanta. I pulled over on the side of the road when I felt your spirit depart this earth. I knew because it departed me. I grabbed the steering wheel, screaming, you were being ripped from my very being. A mother always knows. A mother knows when the baby is entering the world, and she knows when that baby departs even if separated by state lines. I sat, drained. I could feel the life of my only son slipping away.

I pulled into the QuikTrip; my body needed a release. I closed the stall door behind me; my phone began to ring. I fumbled, knowing it was the call. I answered, some nondescript doctor was talking to me, "Ms. Gray, this is doctor…I'm so sorry for your loss." A sledgehammer hit me, knocking the wind from my lungs. My ribs felt as though they were sinking in; from my fingertips to the very pores in my body, every major organ responded in unison. I began to scream "Noooooo, nooooo, Jesus, Jesus, Jesus" as though I was on autopilot. I had to make it to the car; it felt like I was caught in a cyclone that picked me up and hurled me into a warped reality. I had to call your sister and listen to her muffled cries, begging me to be safe. I was in Charlotte, North Carolina, disoriented and confused. I had to make it to the nearest airport.

An eerie calm came over me, and I told myself to make it safely back to the one child I had left. I didn't have a chance to hold your hand and kiss your forehead like I used to when you were troubled. We were separated. Oh my god, separated! Mother and son—not now! Please God, please God, pleeeaaassse…I received comfort from my dear trusted friend, James, who stayed on the phone with me and prayed for me. He said, "I'm going to be on this phone with you until you get on that plane." What an ordeal! I had never left you since you were eight years old. I asked you to come with me, a road trip. You sadly declined, saying you needed to see about your friend, you didn't want to leave him alone. So noble, thoughtful, and caring. You always laid aside your own comfort and desires to accommodate others. Today, those traits will be celebrated because those traits are rare. Unfortunately, we live in a ruthless society where people only care about themselves.

The legacy of your love for others and your ability to rise to greatness will be shared with viewers across Palm Coast, the US, and abroad. You were always the nurturer and a caring person. Firm but fair. I taught you the value of truth and honor. When you were around six, you stole a pack of jawbreakers out of the store (Target). When I got home, they were in the bag with the rest of the grocery items. When I asked you about them and then discovered you stole them, I spanked your behind, put you in the car, and took you back to Target. I made you tell the store manager and the security guard that you stole the candy; they smiled and said, "Aww, that's okay." I was furious! I told them to do their jobs! It was not okay, and as men, they had a responsibility to lead you in the right direction (I told them it takes a village).

The deputy asked me after he looked at your cute almond-shaped eyes, long, thick lashes, and dimples that could charm anyone, "Ma'am, don't you think you are being too harsh?"

I told him, "No, because if he were sixteen, you would wrestle him to the ground, make a scene, handcuff him, and send him off to jail. Now do your job!" I hissed at him between clenched teeth.

He got down on one knee, crisscrossed your little arms—extending them forward—and asked you if you wanted him to put you in handcuffs and take you to jail. You started whimpering, "No, Sir." I told you that you were never to go into a store and leave out with an item without a receipt. You asked me in that upturned cute as a button face, "What's a receipt, Mommy?"

I replied, "A piece of paper that shows you paid and gives you the right to have that treat." I gave you the money and made you place the item on the conveyor belt, and when the cashier gave you the receipt, I said very excitingly, "Look, Curtis, you bought your own candy! That is a receipt!" Your little face was beaming, you were proud. You felt good that you paid for something you wanted. I never had to worry about you stealing again after a few more butt whippings. I was determined I would not raise a criminal, a thief, or a liar under my roof.

Your whole life was built around life lessons, lots of discipline with love and truth! Always own your truth! I didn't have to worry about you not having integrity. I spanked you enough that you understood character and honor had to be your essential traits. I always told you and Destiny whenever you act up; that was when I was going to spank your behind. You all knew not to throw tantrums in public, and you knew not to touch anything in the store. I would hear you guys speaking, and you would say, "Destiny, Mom really does have eyes in the back of her head." Too funny! I kept a close watch over the years and tried to also give you space to make your own decisions, telling you that you would have to own the consequences.

You learned from your dad to blame the world around you. We had to really work on that. I would hold you to task and make you take responsibility for your own actions. You would come up with every excuse why something was someone else's fault. We would go toe-to-toe on that. When you turned eighteen, we had the biggest fight after I took you to get a rental vehicle when you totaled your car. As we were driving away from the rental place, I kicked you out of the car and made you walk home for not having a plan of action. You had wrecked your car; you begged me to come pick you up at the Enterprise. When I got there, you were sitting on the curb because you did not check ahead of time to see if they were open. I was furious because I left my job in the middle of training to accommodate you. I kicked you out of the car on SR 100 and made you walk back home. I told you your lack of planning was not my responsibility, and you needed to own your mistake in not taking all the necessary steps. That was a character flaw embedded deep in you through the example that was left from your dad. I would not give you a pass on lack of ownership! I taught you "real men own up." After that blow-up, you were angry for a minute, but you sent me a text: thanks, Mom, for keeping it 100 percent!

Curtis, with you and Destiny, I felt that integrity and great character would take you both far. It was paramount to me, as your mother, that you embraced your flaws and work on them without salty excuses. You and she pouted, but I was not a tired mom who would cave in and let you have your way. I used to tell you and Destiny all the time, "I'm your mother, not a friend, buddy, or a pal, not your equal, and not to be played with."

You both knew ultimately it was for your own good. I would often hear you tell your friends, "My momma don't play." I am glad, son, that all the tough love paid off.

I knew that if I didn't raise you right, the world would make you pay in ways that could mar your name for life. It was my job to make sure you and Destiny had a good name. I used to tell you, "When you walked out that door, remember, you are a Gray, and you had better not do *anything* I wouldn't approve of." I would ask you, "What's your name?" And then tell you "you'd better recognize" after you stated your name in full. I'm smiling as I'm recalling those moments.

You and Destiny understood integrity was everything. Your character will be approved by those who spend time with you. It doesn't mean you are perfect, but that you are perfectly consistent in showing others who you *really* are. I didn't have to esteem you, nope, my work was behind closed doors. I never took a break, shaping you and molding you. You were by no means perfect, but you remained transparent! What was done behind closed doors was made evident by how you radiated in the community. Your dad taught you disciplines, financial responsibilities, survival skills, and how to be independent. We both taught you the value of having a *good* name.

Well, son, one year has passed, and the measure of your name will be celebrated. The integrity you had will be put on display. All this matters even to the grave because while your earthly body is gone, son, your name lives on.

#LLC

#LongLiveCurt

Long live Curtis Israel Gray! You made your mama proud, baby!

Loving you to infinity and beyond,
Mom

PS: ANGELS, CURT NEEDS THIS LETTER. PLEASE RUSH.

CHAPTER 15

GOOD MORNING, MY SINGING SONNY

GOSH, I MISS YELLING "SONNY" IN the house. You got used to it. Initially, you didn't like it, but your mom always had pet names for you guys. Love ya, babe. For you, it's another day in paradise, and well for me, I'm grinding. My schedule is full today, I have your LLC stop the violence community tournament going on. I anticipate it being a means to unite the community as well as purpose-driven. We are sending a message in solidarity of violence intolerance and positive mental health in the aftermath of tragedy. The goal is to provide the families of this community the necessary resources to help the kids and parents who are grieving to cope with the trauma of your death. Many of the adults are still mourning you, and often, I find I must wrap my arms around them and comfort them. They all say, "You are such a strong woman." I'm not sure how true that is, I crumble in private behind closed doors, feeling most vulnerable and alone at times. If there is a perceived measure of strength, they surely haven't seen me in my weakest moments where my very energy seems to drain from me, leaving me too weak to get out of bed.

Some of the kids are still reeling and are not sure how to cope. It is horrific, the impact this has permanently made in so many lives. You were adored greatly, Sonny, and you are missed; unfortunately, some of the kids are suffering from depression and anxiety. It is my hope that through this "stop the violence" event, we will be able to assist them with some relief from volunteers from the local mental health agencies.

I'm concerned about those who are closest to you, and as often as I can, I send messages of encouragement and love to many of your friends. I also reach out to your adopted family; I thank God for them for coming into your life at a time when it was most needed. You were blessed to have a man who stepped in as a father figure and a woman you adored as a second mother. You were also blessed to have loved completely before your early departure.

Son, I want you to know that the kids are posting songs on Snapchat; apparently, you taught those close to you how to freestyle, singing old-school classics (like New Edition and Adele). Adele! Really? Wow! Your appreciation for music was broad, with genres ranging from gospel to hard rap, jazz, and old-school R&B. You and Destiny gained your love for music from me and your dad. Remember when Destiny fell in love with country music, and she made us listen to it? I still find that humorous, although, truthfully, I like a little country myself at times. Remembering that makes me smile.

I'm trying to recall if there was ever a day that you did not belt out music. You sang with everything you had. I used to stand outside the bathroom and listen to you sing with intent; I would yell through the door, "Sing, baby!" However, for the longest, you would never learn the words, just hollering out the hook over and over again, gosh, how I miss that! We kept the house full of music;

sometimes, your dad would set the keyboard up and just play old-school hits. You guys loved that, and at times, I would crank the volume up loud on YouTube artists I loved, and we would belt out my favorites, Mary J. Blige's "Fine" and Lalah Hathaway's "Angel." You and Dee got used to it, and it was comforting, joyful, and freeing. There was always music in the house.

I was proud when you and your sister joined the jazz band in middle school, each gaining first chair, she as percussionist and you in alto and tenor sax. I especially loved it when you accompanied your dad on sax as he played the keys, you were awesome together. He taught you how to hear the music and pick the notes out by ear. It made my heart swell, and I would say, "Do it again."

Singing came natural for you when you were three years old. Your favorite song was a Barney song, "Clean up, clean up, everybody, everywhere. Clean up, clean up, everybody, do your share." From there, I had high hopes. My baby could sing! By the time you turned six years old, I would encourage those little vocals, always prompting, "Sing, baby, sing." If I encouraged you, you kept belting. You filled our house with song. I can't remember a day when you didn't sing. Not one. You passed that love of music on to your friends. They emulate you still today with your passion for expression through music.

All right, my little Sonny, that's enough for today. I've got work to do; you made me promise to be *great*, so I'm off at it.

I love you to infinity,
Mom

PS: ANGELS, SPEEDY DELIVERY PLEASE.

CHAPTER 16

GOOD MORNING, SON OF MINE

THERE IS something you should know, so many songs have been made about you. They are awesome. You often sang, dragging your dutiful friends into your selection of old-school music, teaching your White friends how to "spit lyrics and freestyle." A lot of them have found their voice and lyrics in music to ease the pain of their loss. The expressions have been powerful. When the news of your death first hit, a lot of the kids took to graphics, loading Twitter with artful reflections of you sprouting angel wings. One of those graphics has forever changed the track uniform for FPCHS. That uniform is being sold to raise monies for the scholarship fund in your name. I know I sent this tidbit of information to you earlier. I like to focus on the positive. It helps my day stay positive. I'm going to send you the song one of your classmates made for you.

Also, I am so glad you captured on video a few of your singing and dancing escapades! Amanda came by last week to show me a video of you and your friend's musical performance outside in front of the garage. Too funny! I loved every minute of how you enjoyed life. You, your friends, and I would ride around, singing to the top of our voices, jamming to old-school music with me screaming, "Y'all don't know nothin' 'bout this. This is when music was real!"

You would groan and say, "Mom, you say this every single time!" But you would be grinning from ear to ear, appreciating the vibe of R&B. You made your guys listen and learn the lyrics to Adele. LOL! Adele, a White, British artist, appreciated by a young Black male… but hey, she could blow indeed! You loved the artist H.E.R. For you, it was about musical composition and lyrics. You had a broad appreciation for great vocalists. You were good in your own right as well.

Remember when you were maybe around nine, I would be yelling enthusiastically "sing, baby, sing?" Destiny would roll her eyes in her head and say, "Mom, don't encourage him." I didn't care, I just loved the fact that you sang from the time you woke up in the morning until you went to bed. Back then, it was a repetition of one line because you wouldn't learn the lyrics (LOL).

I guess me and your dad made you and Destiny appreciate music and develop your repertoire. I really wished you had continued to play the saxophone because were a natural, even able to play by ear. I remember your dad on the keys and you on the sax playing away. That is a memory I will always treasure. When you learned both alto and tenor sax, I thought that was epic! You played on the jazz band at Indian Trails, and boy, was I proud. I still have those photos.

You didn't grow to appreciate that gift because you loved football more! Oh well, but it didn't keep you from turning to your next love: dancing! Remember how many times you tried to teach me how to *dap* or *dab*? I don't know what that crazy dance was…you would get so excited when I could do it, you would put me on Snapchat, *dapping* and *freestyling.* You and Josh would laugh so hard at me trying to rap. Sometimes, it was so lame; and then sometimes, I was able to hit it just right! Yay for mom! Remember when the guys would come to the house and I would be in the kitchen, cooking, you would always try to make me perform in front of your friends? Too funny! What great memories, kiddo, what great memories.

Hey, by the way, you had an inkling to show off all your baby-and-up photos from that scrapbook I was working on. I can't find that book anywhere. I told you to be sure not to lose it. TG says he doesn't know what you did with it. I couldn't find it, and I told you specifically those were all the photos I had of you and not to misplace them. I am hoping someone didn't do something with them deliberately. I have searched everywhere, and I can't find them *anywhere.* I am so disappointed; I need those pictures! I don't want to grow old and have nothing to reflect on. I want to remember every smile, every birthday, your kindergarten graduation, every honor roll certificate, and the family moments we shared. Those things are irreplaceable. If you know where it is, I need a sign. I'm just saying, do something, please. I need them! I know that sounds ridiculous, but it's a simple request.

Anyway, you know if you were still here, I would have yelled your ear off for losing that scrapbook, and I would have made you search every cranny for it, but honestly, I believe it was destroyed deliberately. I don't want to think that, but sometimes, when people don't have what you have, jealousy manifests in crazy ways. I try not to think about it. It makes me sad.

Son, I don't know what your days and nights are like in heaven, but I'm sure you are surely teaching the angels moves, and knowing you, you have probably rearranged the music in heaven to replicate a little R&B or rap (SMH). You made everyone around you sing (LOL)! Even the nonsingers.

In your honor at the memorial, we sang your all-time favorite "Can You Stand the Rain" by New Edition. We waved our arms in the air and sang it at the top of our voices, "Sunny days, everybody loves them, but baby, can you stand the rain?" I can't sing that song without tearing up. I love that you loved that. The lyrics mean something so deep. I feel that you could appreciate them because of everything you had to overcome. Wow! Even as I am typing, I am reflecting on the lyrics. It was everything you and the ones you loved went through together. It was the cliff-hanging relationship you had with your father, and the disappointment you experienced with friends who parted ways with you and crushed your heart. Those relationships dated back to middle school.

By the way, many came to the house after the news of your death. Your longtime comrade cried so much, he felt horrible. I told him it was okay; I held him close at your grave site and told him you had already forgiven him and that you loved him like a brother. He cried in my neck, and I rocked him like a baby. Your capacity to forgive was great; it was indeed your strength. Son, you were loved like a brother, I'm sure you know that. His mom asked permission to put flowers on your grave while I was at the graduation; I told her, "Absolutely!" So many people loved you, li'l guy.

Well, sweetie, I have to begin my day. You know I love you in a million plus ways. You are my son. The only one I have, and you were awesome at being a great son. I will always be appreciative for the treasure that was in you. One last little surprise, that single you were waiting on from Destiny came back. Your auntie Judith loves it! She listens to it all the time. Powerful lyrics but you should have kept them clean. If you were alive, I would have made you redo it by expanding your vocabulary. Yep, that's right! You already know how I feel about that, however, lyrically, it was masterful. Judith had to explain to me that the lyrics were a metaphorical expression about your entrance into the world of music! I was like, "Ohhh." She said any artist and anyone in the music industry would understand the metaphor of the lyrics and know that you were singing about debuting yourself as a new up-and-coming artist and the hustle and drive you had to put into creating the music. The kids love it. As your mom, I want to tell you I'm proud that you took a chance to do something you loved.

Nothing but love, boy, nothing but love,
Mom

CHAPTER 17

GRATEFUL TO BE GREAT

HEY, son of mine! Remember how I kept a gratitude journal, logging nightly at least three things I was grateful for? I opened it last week and saw my last log was on April seventh. You departed this temporary life into eternity on April thirteenth, and I noticed that the journaling came to an abrupt halt. No more written gratitude. It was swallowed up in immeasurable grief. It was engulfed by indescribable disabling pain that consumed my days and nights but fueled me into action to make something positive of your memory for those you left behind. Now that energy that surged into your DNA from mother to son boomeranged right back to me with the compelling challenge you left behind when you said to me, "Ma, choose something and be great. Promise me you will be great." You then said, "I know I'm going to be great."

I responded, "Yes, you will, son, you certainly will." It was a conversation between two souls understanding the language spoken was eternal and not relegated to mere words, anchoring a hope to a future in which your greatness would be revealed without you living in your mortal body. A conversation that was being recorded in the eons of eternity, hurled into the atmosphere with a promise between mother and son to "be great." It was an inner understanding that the challenge would be life-altering, changing, and evolving into the unknown. A journey in which I would walk alone without the presence of my challenger.

In the moment of that conversation, you chided me for being a fifty-year-old woman working at a regular job, dabbling in various ventures but not settling on one thing to be great. I remember the gut-punch effect that must have registered on my face because you said to me, "Ma, I know this must be hard to hear, but who else will tell you this?" You went on to say, "Now don't go getting all in your feelings. It has to be me." Then you smiled that deep simple smile to soften the blow as I allowed the words to marinate a little bit. In that moment, my pride set me back a little because, as your mother, what I heard you saying was that you were waiting to see greatness emerge from me.

Up to this point, I had only been exemplifying subpar normalcy, going through the mundane nuances of working a job that would not make room for the gifts you knew I possessed. You wanted more from your mother, pushing me the way you pushed yourself to emerge past depression, pushing yourself to increase your body strength to overcome the weakness you suffered in your body post broken bones, a torn hip flexor, and the impact of a wreck—all the while pushing yourself to live up to your fullest potential. You needed me to "be great." Being great became your focus, it became a part of your daily conversation. You said to me, "I know I'm going to be great. I know I will pursue a career in the stock market." You gave me that heartwarming smile.

I gave you my mother talk with lots of emphasis, "Yes, you will, boy. Yes, you will!"

We stood there appreciating each other in the way that we had become very comfortable with. Our conversations in the last few months of your life had more depth. We were pushing each other to the intended outcome of our lives, nudging each other's souls to become the better part of ourselves. I felt my greatest accomplishment as your mom would be to send you out successfully ready for college, the next chapter of your life.

Destiny's emergence into life seemed to take a lot less effort. My words to her seemed to travel a shorter distance and resonating in a way that clicked. With you, your male component mixed with the complexity of your profound maturity always seemed to provide a longer path to travel. The distance of our language was throwing up detours and roadblocks along the way. However, we had somehow managed to understand each other's language through lots of tears, misunderstandings, and the practice of listening over the last several months of your life; and as we stood in the kitchen that day, I heard you. "Mom, promise me you will be great." I thank you for that; I wake up with it as my internal GPS daily. That promise I made to you was captured by the universe, recorded by heaven, and noted by my soul and spirit—that I would indeed strive for greatness.

Curtis, listen to me, I was expressive with you from the time you were an infant. When you were a toddler, I always spoke to you in a way that challenged you to learn more and learn quicker. You began speaking full sentences at the age of fifteen months old. You held amazing conversations at the age of four. I would always challenge your vocabulary and made you expand your word usage. When you were only six years old, you became momma's great little sales person, working business-to-business sales with me for my company, Yellow Book. I would take you with me to close a sale. Honestly, I wasn't the best salesperson, but you had that splendid round face, beautiful brown skin, and deep dimples. You would smile big and bright, holding that phone book in front of your chest, and when the business owner would come to greet me, you would say with exuberance, "Hi, my name is Curtis, and I'm with Yellow Book." We closed so many sales! Always the consummate team, baby, you and me.

Just as I was expressive with you, I allowed you and your sister to be expressive with me. I remember when we were at 77 Fortress Place, you taught me the art of listening. It was a lesson I will cherish for the rest of my life. You had a way of shutting down on me when we would have intense conversations. It always offended me, and then one night, you explained to me that when you are talking, if I interrupted you, it would cause your brain to shut down, lose your original thought, and then cause you to be frustrated as a result of that interruption. You made me understand what you needed from me as your mom. I felt that night was a huge hurdle for us. We had come to place a common ground, and from there, we could build upon a solid foundation of mutual understanding and respect. That night, I verbally shared with you that parents don't have it all figured out; and for me, I felt honored that you trusted me enough to share your vulnerability with me.

Up until that point, I didn't understand the language barrier. We talked about how I implemented the same behaviors to you and your sister that were passed on to me from my mother, and it was ineffective for you guys. My mother raised us not to have the last say. Her statements usually ended with "because I said so." It was my norm, and it created inner turmoil for me because I was a child who needed to communicate my feelings without the fear of being punished. That night, I apologized to you; I realized that for seventeen years, I had been stifling the conversations you desired to have with your mom, it made me feel sick, my gut turned. I was repeating the same behavior that drove a wedge between me and mom. I wanted better for us.

The art of listening is essential for any relationship to blossom. It became my goal after our conversation: to develop the art of listening. It was your gift, and it benefitted many. You were slow to speak, always churning your words before releasing the value of them loosely. Your friends found comfort in your sage wisdom; they looked to you for guidance and leadership. You were a beacon for many of them in their own turbulent situations. I believe that listening was indeed one of your greatest assets. It took a while because I finally got it. You challenged me to "be great," and I heard you with my inner ear. It echoes in my spirit daily. Its rhythmic flow and cadence bouncing around in my heart keeps me focused; it is the premise for the decisions I make and the connections I choose. I've decided that those in my inner circle must be willing to appreciate that greatness and embrace their own. You would always say, "If you're going to do something, don't be average, be great." I will, baby. I will be great at journaling the things I am grateful for again. I will be great at building your foundation to help other families walking through dark traumas. I will continue to be great at being yours and Destiny's mom.

I love you, my guy! You and your sister are my treasures, and for that, I am truly grateful!

With love,
Mom

PS: ANGELS, SPECIAL DELIVERY.

CHAPTER 18

HEAVEN

HEY, li'l dude, what's happening? Who's keeping up with your hair in heaven? What do you eat? Do you laugh? What's the music like? How many angels have you met? Is there a fragrance in heaven like honey-suckle or jasmine or lavender or perhaps magnolia? What about the colors? Can you name them? Can you see the Milky Way? Is there special lighting in heaven? Do they give off a different brilliance? Are there ever nap times or sleep? Do you drink water from fountains? Or does heaven have goblets made from opulent jewels? Are there clouds and rainbows? What animals are in heaven? Do they have the need to chew grass, eat herbs, and lay in dewy beds of lush green?

Let's talk about temperature. Is it cool, mild, balmy, or tropical without the excessive heat? Freshwater or saltwater? Are there springs and rivers, waterfalls and foamy currents? Do the birds chirp and sing beautifully? Do they dance with butterflies? Do you hear the laughter of chubby giggly babies, cooing and making smacking baby noises? Who changes their diapers? Huh? Never thought about that. Does heaven come equipped with hammocks, lullabies, and blissful, peaceful days full of languid, easy conversations among family, friends, the twelve apostles, and twenty-four elders?

Are God's eyes kind and gentle? What does he smell like? Does his voice rumble when he speaks? Or is it soft and gentle like granddad's with a deep but beautiful vibrato? Does he enjoy humor and laughter? When he laughs, does it come from deep within, booming and contagious? Is he proud of you? Do you make him smile?

Remember to always say "yes, Sir" and "thank you" when you talk to him. Please tell him I appreciate his love for you and us. Tell him I'm so happy he gave you dimples (that was a nice touch). It's the little things, you know. Tell him the smile was a bonus, totally infectious and winning! Great job on that one! Tell him I still feel jaded on the shortened life span, but I really need his help in coping with that reality. I relive it every day, and it's challenging, but I'd like to think that he allows you to swim to your heart's content, run down the streets of gold, and play air football with the angels (you, the quarterback). I can live with that—with you playing without pain, having endless victories, and being safe and secure in his care for all eternity. I guess that's kind of fair. I still am working through it in my humanity.

I'll bet when God smiles, no matter where you are in the courts of heaven, it changes everything. The angels fly with more vigor, the birds sing a little louder, perhaps the clouds sway and dip, the rainbow's colors are more vivid, and the rushing water sings a melody. I would be willing to bet that he lent you some of that, my boy, because when you smiled, it changed the atmosphere. In every interview, the kids and teachers said, "When Curt smiled, it lit up the room." I now know that was part of your gift. You changed the atmosphere with your smile, knocking darkness into oblivion.

You were executed with a smile on your face. I know this because I asked the kids if there was any hostility or words exchanged on the night of your death. They said, "No, Ms. Carmen, we assumed Curtis was flirting with that girl because when she said to him, 'Looks like you want some smoke.' He just laughed." They saw you smiling. Your friends will have that smile (the essence of who you were) stamped in their memory forever!

I believe that when you smiled, it brought healing to you first and then to others around you. It was a reassurance that things were going to be all right. Now the angels and the hosts of heaven are blessed to have you smiling in their presence, flashing those beautiful teeth and deep dimples. Oh, by the way, are your ears still pierced and studded with brilliant stones more precious than diamonds? Just curious. I believe if God accepts you as you are on earth, he just upgrades you when you get to heaven (just sayin').

All right, my baby, my eyes are heavy, I didn't sleep well last night. I toss and turn every night, and the saga continues into the next day. I am going to try to rest now if I can. I love you to the moon and back, but that has limits, so I love you to eternity and whatever else goes with that. You are a part of me, we shared the same body for the miraculous space of nine months. Perhaps, you need to talk to God about the mystery of childbearing…okay, never mind. I will ask him myself. All right, all right, I'm bringing this to a close because you would be saying to yourself "oh my gosh, Mom, I am not going to ask him that" with a crazy grin on your face, rolling your eyes in your head and muttering out loud, "Really?"

So for now no more questions or interrogation, I'm letting you off easy. I'm sure you thought leaving earth would relieve you from my constant barrage of questions, but unfortunately, for you, there is no escape. You will always receive these text messages from me, and yes, you must read them. I made a deal with God many years ago when I was seven years old. He always hears my prayers, so if he can't escape, neither can you.

With love,
Mom

PS: ANGELS, Y'ALL ALREADY KNOW I NEED A SPECIAL DELIVERY, PLEASE. (LOOK, SON, EVEN THEM KNOW.)

CHAPTER 19

HEY, BOY!

GUESS WHAT? I am working out now! Coach Chris has been coming to the house to help me and Dee work the stress out of our bodies! I found out yesterday that lifting weights eliminates depression and anxiety. This was a method you used to deal with the stress of me and your dad's divorce. That was smart, and now I'm following the example you left behind. I must do self-help because the attorney general's office is running into static, trying to get help for me and your sister. I hope your days are filled with unspeakable joy and full of God's glory! I hope that you know Destiny and I will be all right. We have faith in God, and we have a lot of people praying for us, including your teachers, friends, and even the superintendent. He and his wife are awesome people, and they have supported us 100 percent. He prays for me and Destiny all the time. We are surrounded with support from the community, our family members—near and far— and from my customers. I went to your old job; your boss, Tony, expressed his condolences and talked about what an amazing worker you were and how he admired your commitment to work while playing sports. They really appreciated you there.

Well today's letter is short; I just wanted to let you know that I could feel you cheering me and Dee on yesterday as we worked out. I told Coach Chris you would be cheering us on, and he said you would have told him, "Nah, Unk, work them a little harder." I said to him that sounds exactly like something you would be saying, but you would be grinning that grin of yours with those deep dimples.

Love you, boy of mine,
Mom

PS: Angels, this is a special delivery. Be sure to get this to him, please.

CHAPTER 20

I Release You, My Baby

CURTIS ISRAEL GRAY, you are my beloved son in whom I am well pleased. You have brought me joy in so many ways from the time you came out of my womb with your face stretched wide, stained red from wailing. You made an entrance into my life with one foot carefully dislodged from under my ribs. I not so politely inquired of your obstetrician, "Where is the rest of him?" He assured me he would eventually get you out. I watched the clock tick; thirty minutes had passed. I was getting nervous because with my first surgical excursion of birth, your sister was scalped out within five minutes. However, you were a new millennium baby who arrived via laser surgery. I soon learned the laser procedure took a little longer. Your dad fainted at the sight and the smell of burning flesh, but then, somehow, you emerged unscathed in all your bountiful presence, belting out your entrance into this world on a beautiful morning of December 11, 2000. I knew then you would be special.

Throughout preschool and kindergarten, you shone and radiated with that wide, beaming smile, and all your teachers loved you. I remember your kindergarten graduation, you in that little blue cap and gown, singing with your classmates and grinning so proudly as you belted out your words, swaying and grinning. I remember you were a turkey in your Thanksgiving play. I arrived late due to work, and you were very upset with me. It was then that I vowed I would make you and your sister my priority. I remember that sickening feeling of having disappointed you like it was yesterday. However, even though I was late, I was a proud, proud mama. When you were six, I started teaching you "acting lessons" by having you perform impromptu skits. Those events with you and your sister were fun and always made my chest swell a bit because I was certain you would become a child star. Those were lofty dreams, and life was beautiful and full of possibilities for you and your sister. The thought of that makes me smile.

You were well-loved by the neighbors of Town Square, it is a community full of caring neighbors where each adult understands fully that it does take a village to raise one child. You and Destiny were blessed to have the privilege of safety, and you all understood the fundamental value of community. I reflect on how respectful and helpful you were with the neighbors. I am so glad your dad invested time to teach you how to mow the lawn, hunt, fish, wash the car, and be a responsible young man. Those were great days, son, days that I fondly remember. You made so many beautiful deposits into my life, and I treasure the many memories. You never brought me any pain or heartache. You were loving, kind, thoughtful, genuinely caring, giving, and very obedient. I couldn't ask for a better son. You knew how to honor your parents and those in authority; you remained honorable even until the time of your departure.

I can now let you rest in peace because you have earned it, my son. You did what you came to do. Your assignment was fulfilled, and you did it with such grace. I want you to know your labor here is done, and you worked well and pleasing to God and also to me, your mother. I crown you with all the love a mother can give her one and only son, and I bid you farewell for now until the time we are rejoined for eternity. I am not saying goodbye for we shall see each other again. I loved you in life, and I love you in death. Your life brought me immeasurable joy, and I want you to know that Destiny and I will get through this together. We will heal, and we shall see you again, son, when God so chooses. I know that he will unite us again, and it will be a happy reunion. I pray your father turns his life over to God as well. God is able.

For you, my dear boy,
Mom

PS: ANGELS, RUSH DELIVERY, PLEASE.

CHAPTER 21

I AM YOUR MOTHER

LITTLE BOY, I hate to think that the ending of your life is the beginning of mine. Carmen Alexis Gray exists no more, rather, just Carmen Alexis, redefining a future without a son in her present. Perhaps, however, you and I are blending, merging as one. Could it be that just as a mother carries a child in her body to bring it into the world, perhaps when the child departs the world in which he entered, he reenters his destiny through the same portal from his origin? Or is it the desperate hope of a mother not wanting one piece of her child to leave her behind empty? I have to hope that while your physical body is gone, spirit-to-spirit we will always be connected. I am your mother, destined by God to carry you, nurture you, bury you, memorialize you, and entrust you into his eternal care. You were simply on loan to me for a while. For eighteen amazing years, I was trusted by the one who created you to teach you, chastise you, and raise you up to be who you were created to be.

I had to pay attention and observe and guide you in the way you should go. Sometimes, I misunderstood, but you made sure I kept up with the original blueprint and did not falter from the architectural design of who you were destined to be. You were not afraid to embrace your gifts, although it took a little nudging. At times, you felt challenged and insecure by your sister, Destiny's academic focus and determination. I told you to find what you were good at and be the best in that area, and that only you could fulfill the purpose you were supposed to manifest. It resonated with you, settling upon you like a well-worn garment. You embraced that notion, and it caused you to refocus and discover Curtis the leader, not the follower.

Destiny often marveled at your brilliance, stating in amazement that the things that challenged her academically came natural to you in Math and Science. You were an A honor roll student until you were distracted with the faltering of our family dynamics, but you found your way again within the last months before you transitioned. You also understood that without asking for the role of a leader, it was entrusted to you; we had many conversations about that and what it meant to lead when no one was watching and what it would cost you even if it meant losing friends. You are still leading even in your physical absence. Greatness resonates in your name, leaving a mark that can't be erased, "prince among men."

I am humbled that you are my son, conflicted at times at the shortened life span but knowing you also carried a maturity that most men three times your age did not possess. I am your mother. Sometimes, lost; sometimes, humored by a memory; sometimes, longing to hold you again; sometimes, bereft in grief; sometimes, lonely for the comfort your presence brought especially when you would come to my room to make sure I was "tucked" in; sometimes, shielded by your protective nature; sometimes, proud of the nobility of your character; and sometimes, reminded of your emergence into manhood and the conflict it yielded because you didn't fully understand that being a man required discipline. I remember when you turned eighteen, I admonished you that you could no longer vacillate between being a boy and a man when it was convenient for you, that you had to choose. I told you that you would no longer be able to hide behind excuses nor blame others for your mistakes, but as a man, you would have to take full responsibility for your actions. You gravely accepted the weight of that awareness and tried to live up to it.

I write these things to you because it is important for you to know that I saw you, son. I know you wondered if I noticed. I did. Your efforts to obey, the seeds you sowed still bear fruit. You did well, and you were relentlessly trying to show me who you were. I saw you, baby, with eyes wide open, mom saw you. The time now is 2:26 a.m. You used to come to me and ask me, "Ma, why are you still up?" Old habits die hard for sure. I stayed up with you when you were in my womb, therefore, sometimes, I'm up because it's in the stillness of the night that I can feel your presence, and it's in the late nights when the awareness of your absence keeps me awake. While I miss your beautiful smile, the deep rumble of laughter in your chest, the dimples, and glistening white smile, I imagine that through the vapor of eternity, we still occupy space together, mother and son.

I told you and Destiny many times I would gladly endure all the pain again to have you both in my life. I have mothered you without regret except the early departure. I needed more time. More time for deep penetrating discussions on life, more time for discovery and adventure, more time to watch you make "manly" decisions—as you would like to call them—more time to turn the volume of the music up, more time to laugh over silly memories, more time to remind you "boy, I will chop you in your throat," more time to cheer from the sidelines, more time to hear you call me mother, mommy, or ma, and more time to watch you swallow life in deep gulps of air. You were passionate about everything—everything representing an embodiment of explosive energy and life, an abrupt eruption in the mundane nuances of life. When you were knocked off your axis, you found your way back by God's Grace. It was profound to watch you rise up from despair and then help others.

God gifted you, blessed you, and took you when he saw fit. I will be forever grateful that I was the one chosen to bring you into the world. I've had a lot of time to reflect one year post your death, and it is evident to me that God's sovereignty is without question, his love unfailing, his ways are far above ours, and, ultimately, he knows the plans that he has for us. I can say this now and not feel the bile rise in my throat (at least not in this moment).

Grief is tricky and blinding at times; it's like being at the mercy of a never-ending body of water. You can't predict the waves. Sometimes, the water seems placid; at other times, the force of grief can feel like a tsunami. So here I sit, in another form of grief, writing while my body bears the awful pain of your loss. No pill can ease the ache; no sleeping aid can lure me away from the ever-present awareness of the void that occupies the space you once inhabited. I focus now on your sister to make sure she is well because the loss is not easy to accept. However, the clock is ticking; and sometimes, the best way for me to cope is to slip into another day, so I will lay my body down, my baby, perhaps you will come see your mother in a dream even if it's just for a fleeting moment.

Ask God for me to allow you passage into my dreams; it's a small request.

I love you, mama's boy,
Mom
XOXOXO

CHAPTER 22

KINGDOM CREED: JUST BE GREAT

HEY, baby guy! I slept in this morning until 10:20 a.m.! Yikes, now I feel slow and sluggish. Missing you with extreme everything! My baby. My guy. My treasure. This is hard on so many levels. I am really struggling to keep it together. People look at me and use the word "strong." They don't see all the little fragments and powder dust left in your wake!

A boy who wanted to make a name for himself and placement in a gang killed a part of me when he killed you. He killed your children, killed your future and every promise of hope. What an ignorant and arrogant way to excel. He excelled in death—a very permanent position he will hold for the rest of his unfulfilled sorry life—wayward and desolate, shadowed by darkness and no hope, soulless and sullied, marred by the wrong decision to be great. Funny, two young men striving for greatness: one following a path of light and the other in pursuit of darkness.

Your motto "Just be great" has covered the airways; it has been rehearsed from your lips to your peers, from your peers among themselves, and from your heart to your mother. You wore it on your clothing. It was your creed, just like in Medieval days a king/prince always lives by a creed. It was the emblem of their kingdom, and all the kingdom knew the creed. Anyway, I'm cutting this short for now.

I TRIED TO SEND YOU SOMETHING JUST NOW, AND IT DID not send. I hope you get this!

Love,
Mom

CHAPTER 23

LEGACY BIRTHER

TODAY, I awakened with the keen sense of your departure. You were born to a scheduled surgical procedure on December eleventh. I waited patiently through the laser procedure; your dad fainted at the sight of the instruments. At 8:35 a.m. you emerged, wailing with lungs full of life and strength. Your latte skin, dark, swathing hair, deep baby dimples, and wide mouth greeted me on a warm Florida December morning. My son, my prince, I promise I celebrate you.

I am a legacy birther. I can tell you I would have never chosen this as my path, but I find myself here on a long, winding road for which I had no clue that your legacy would ultimately be my destiny. This journey has many challenges; the course is winding and lonely at times. The stretch marks you left behind are a reminder that I birthed greatness into this world, and as symbolically as you have stretched my womb, my life is now being stretched, etched forever with the reminder that in my womb, laid a prince; but in the tomb, now lies a king. But in eternity, the king is now in the presence of the King of Kings who predestined his life.

I am intentionally healing along with your sister. It is necessary for the journey that is ahead. While I miss you dearly, I am aware that you left a lot behind for me and your sister to finish. By God's grace and help, I will. I remember how you carried each of your friends closely in your heart and how you cared deeply about making a difference and being great and how you would help the elderly and serve the poor and needy. You had a heart of compassion that made active room for continued service, and you did it all with that winning smile of yours. When you were eight years old, you went missing for about five hours, I panicked and alerted the entire subdivision. I was livid, but you were helping an elderly lady remove the installation out of her attic. Installation removal at eight years old! I was frantic!

You would always stay behind and clean up after youth meetings, picking up the trash and making sure everything was tidy before leaving. Your coaches could always count on you for fundraising; you walked into many subdivisions, meeting the neighbors and knocking on every door. You helped many people relocate and move, and you always made time for small talk with the elderly, cutting their grass if needed or doing miscellaneous chores. Many nights, you left the house to walk a friend through a crisis, telling me, "Ma, I have to do this." You brought many kids across my threshold to offer them a hot meal, shelter, refuge, and counsel.

I used to tell you all the time, "Curtis, you can't save the world." But you tried. Boy, did you try! You made such a huge impact, son, in such a short time! You left your mama proud, baby. I celebrate you, your life, your legacy, your love and contributions to the world you left behind.

On the night of your death, you stopped to help a young man in need. I am glad that you were in your element of helping as you departed this earth. It was your signature. You remained true to who you were even till the last breath. Yes, son, you are departed but never forgotten. I do indeed celebrate you, my son, my prince, my promise.

Eternally,
Mom (legacy birther)

CHAPTER 24

LI'L DUDE

HEY, what are you doing? It's almost midnight (three minutes till). I am tapping away the restlessness that's in my heart. Another night of staying up late, thinking about you. I yearn for my baby; I hear every bump in the house and know that I am alone. My room is illuminated by one lamp; my mattress is indented with the same nightly habit of me sitting by the nightstand, hoping you will come home. My world feels full of unanswered hope. I wonder, *Where did I go wrong? What did I do to warrant such reward?* The sting of the death of my only son, the death of a twenty-two-year marriage, and the death of many dreams of a future with you and the family you were supposed to have.

When you were fifteen, you said, "Ma, you're not going to have to worry about me. I had a dream I married a girl who was mixed." I gave you that "oh, please" look, and you said, "Not White and Black mixed but maybe Hispanic and Black." I cocked my head to the side and asked you how you knew, and you said, "Because her hair was really thick and curly, and her complexion was like she might be Latina." And I was like "huh." You then said you knew you would have no need to worry about money because you were going to make it in the financial world, selling stock or something like that. I pondered that. Then when you met the girl of your dreams, I asked you if you remembered your dream, and you had totally forgotten it, but I had not, I had tucked it away in my heart. But anytime you dreamed anything, I knew it would come to pass. You tried to tell me you dreamed of your death, and I didn't want to hear it because I was afraid it too would come to pass, and it did. My, my, my, now I have to type out a message to you and hope that God, in his mercy (since he took you from me), would at least allow me to connect with you still via text. It's a hope, one of the few I have left.

I heard you, baby. I just didn't want to.

Okay, son, here's the deal, if my texts are reaching heaven, I know they are, I must submit them with the right attitude. No more feeling sorry for myself. You were with me for eighteen beautiful years! I thank God for that! You decided to honor your parents even when you were provoked. I thank God for that. You were an amazing brother to Destiny! I am so thankful to God for that. You found a way to forgive your dad, me, and others who disappointed you. I thank God for that! You used your smile unknowingly to bring such joy into people's lives. I thank God for that. You were determined to live your life to the fullest, helping others work through their own issues. I thank God for that. You came into this life with a purpose, and you maxed it out, boy! I thank God for that. I am grateful to him that your legacy is felt in the hearts of many and will continue to live on. I am grateful that I want to heal to help others.

(God, help my light shine as only you can. Help me praise you through the grief. Thank you for my children, the fruit of my womb. Thank you for every good memory and for the life lessons along the way. Thank you for allowing me to see that I suffer from rejection, and it caused my children to suffer, but you are revealing my broken places. Thank you for giving me a son who would challenge those areas that needed work and a daughter who constantly reminded me of my flaws.)

Son, I ask that you forgive me for the wasted time when I didn't hear because I wasn't listening. It was something you always challenged me on. I have to get better at talking less about me and intentionally listening. It was something you mastered in your few years on the earth. Listening is a great skill set (and you mastered it). Listening skills suggest you have a genuine care about what is in someone else's heart. I am still broken in that area, but you showed me how important it is. I hope to one day be as intentionally attentive as you.

I miss you, child teacher. You taught me so much, and I will always be grateful for those exchanges we had. I will cherish every memory, every dip of your head when you smiled that little sheepish grin you had, every little dance step, every little falsetto as you sang, the way you called me mother when you were being baneful or the way you called me mommy when you wanted mama's love. I miss doting on you, you were my baby, my last born, my only son, the one I knew I had a chance of losing. I wish I had more time, but since I did not, I will be sure to express my gratitude for every second I had with you even when we didn't agree. I treasure every single moment, every single one! Thank you for all the times you said you loved me. Thank you for all the hugs and kisses and words of appreciation. Thanks for being my son. You were amazing at being my Curtis Israel Gray. You are my li'l dude always, and I wouldn't trade a moment. I feel privileged to have raised such a prince, an ambassador. It was an honor to be your mom.

With love,
Mom

PS: Angels, rush delivery!

CHAPTER 25

LITTLE BOY, IF THESE WALLS COULD TALK

HEY, what's up, my son? I visited your casket in my dream the other night, remembering what it was like when I stood over your lifeless body on April twenty-eighth. Your hands were cold to the touch. Your complexion darkened due to the two-week effects of the embalming. The kids looking at you were in shock and many screamed, running out the door from the sheer unbelievable magnitude of your death. It was surreal.

I was escorted for the final viewing of your lifeless body, and a myriad of thoughts crossed my mind. I thought about how loving you were, how you respected me and your father, how you loved your sister, and what a good son you had been. I thought about the loss your death would mean to our future. I could not believe that I would say farewell to the prince I birthed so soon. I couldn't believe that 350 guests would have tear-stained eyes glued to my back as they sadly watched me bid you farewell. My son, my rock, my treasure, my promise, you were loaned out to me with an expiration of eighteen years. I promised God in front of witnesses eighteen years prior as your father and I christened you that I would give you back to God. I'm glad I did. He took great care of you, and he is still taking care of you, my baby.

I felt slighted because I believed you would die an old man with many grandchildren gathered around your bed. Oftentimes, I would tell you that, and you would shake your head no. You knew your time was short, and you did not waste it. You worked tirelessly to impact the lives of your peers, changing the community you left behind one life at a time. You knew, and you wanted me to know. I just didn't want to accept that as your fate. Not my son. Not my baby! Gone too soon, I wasn't ready for your exodus! I needed more time. Your hands were cold, but I laid my hands over those fingers I loved so much, wishing I could, once again, wake you with kisses like I did when you were younger, waking you up with "sticky fingers" like I did when you were seven years old. You would giggle with glee and say, "Mom, do sticky fingers again!" Like, once again, when you were seventeen, I would lay beside you and pray in your ear that God would bless and keep you. I bellowed at you to awaken from a solid sleep after your eighteenth birthday, and you went, "Mom, you don't have to yell. I'm getting up. Oh my god!"

I knew when I gazed upon you, there would be no more FaceTime dates in the grocery store, with you having me scan the aisles for you to shop for the cereal you wanted. No more FaceTime for you to show me what you were cooking or proof that you cleaned your room. No more fighting about me folding up your laundry while you secretly filmed me and put me on Snapchat. No more late-night dancing in the kitchen to the oldies. No more high-pitched singing, "I love you-oooo for so many reasons, and I love you-ooo for so many reasons." Gosh, I miss us laughing about crazy stuff, like when you were telling me you were a man now because you made your own dental appointment (but you needed my insurance card). Me fussing about paying your car insurance. I miss it all, son. I miss you dancing those dances in all your videos, and I miss the twinkle in your eyes when you talked about your future.

I cried so many tears today because I'm leaving all those memories of us in a house that was our fresh start, one we built into a home with the hope of a new beginning. The home that—for you, Destiny, and myself—represented a clean slate, a fresh start after having gone through a hellacious, deceptive marriage and after having gone through the impact the departure of your father had on you and your sister. We were happy here in this house. It was our refuge, a place of healing and peace. You were so happy here; your wounds healed in this house, filled with love and a dream of a brighter tomorrow. It represented the renewal of a relationship between a mother and son that was frayed and tattered by the lies and deceit of a weak and broken man. It was in this house that we learned to talk and listen to each other, discover truths and mend broken fences. In this house, you understood the importance of having an authentic relationship with God. In this house, you bought kids who needed a chance to have hope again. In this house, you built up other young men who were hurting and needed a safe place. In this house, you found your strength, and you gave others a safe place to be.

As your mother, I watched you help so many kids and give them support and a shoulder if they needed one. This house is where the test became your testimony. You are no longer here, son, and if the walls could talk, they would echo all the singing and the many conversations between a mother and her son and the admonishment to live honorably. It would echo out the laughter and the pain and the words of encouragement. It would echo out the disciplines and the pushback from a seventeen-year-old boy navigating his way into manhood. It would echo all the prayers murmured in the still of the night for a son and daughter from a mother whose entire goal was to raise up children to honor God. If these walls could talk, they would echo all the many times the words I love you were spoken freely full of life and hope. If these walls could talk, you would hear the sound of my guttural cry on the nights I have missed you so desperately. They would ooze out the anguish of the pain that erupts loudly, bouncing with a crescendo that clashes into somber silence and hushed whispers of incoherent trauma.

You are the essence of the home we shared, and with your departure, I too am departing soon to go and be with your sister who has suffered in silence, bearing the weight of your tragedy in her body. I want to thank you, son, for making this house the best home for me and your sister. Well done, my baby, well done. Our days here are few; I will start afresh in just a week. It's time for me and Destiny to heal; you will go with me into our new life. You will never be forgotten, my son; your legacy will live on through the seeds you have planted in the lives of many in this town, in this nation, and overseas. I love you, my boy. Thank you for being my son.

With love,
Mom

PS: RUSH DELIVERY, PLEASE.

CHAPTER 26

MEMOIR FROM MOM TO SON

GOOD MORNING, li'l guy! I know you hate it when I call you that. This morning is very difficult. I know now that you really are not coming back. My eyes are laden with tears, and life is bleak. My heart crackles from the immense loss that will never be filled. You are my son, a part of my essence and very being. I write these words, hoping that heaven has some technology to get a message to you, one filled with love and appreciation for a sweet young man with an infectious smile and a heart full of love for humanity.

The other day, I wondered how many mothers birth legends. I don't know the number, but I know the privilege and the pain. Legends can only become legendary at the point of death. There is an exchange of the greatness exemplified on earth for the continued memory of one's contribution, but it can only be obtained in death. It doesn't seem fair. Your contribution in eighteen years will continue to unfold in generations to come. I have had many parents whose homes you have been in tell me what a wonderful difference you have made in their lives and the lives of their children. This impact will reach the next generation and the next. I knew when I held you on the morning of December eleventh that you were destined to do great things. With you, son, I used my words a lot to affirm the man you were becoming. I have no regrets because I never held back. I would rehearse in your ears as I kissed your face and forehead that you would be great and that your life would make a difference. I told you often that I "liked" you, that you made me proud, and that I admired your strength. I encouraged you to take ownership of your mistakes and to release unforgiveness toward your dad for his brokenness. I watched you do it and soar beyond the failure of a man you outgrew through no fault of his own. Life stunted him, but he gave you everything he could until he couldn't. I admonished you to appreciate the good that your father did provide you: shelter, provision, skills, and your musical talent, and he never abused you or your sister. His contribution in your life helped shape you into the competent young man you were. He taught you character in the early years, and that was important. He taught you how to work on a car, cut the grass, tinker with things to build. (Remember the outdoor kitchen he built from scratch?) He taught you how to fish, hunt, swim, and camp. He taught you about having a relationship with God. All was not lost. You blossomed into a beautiful prince. Your name, Curtis Israel Gray, characterized who you were on the earth. Curtis means courteous; Israel means prince among men. You were indeed, son, a courteous prince among men. What a powerful attribute to the legacy you left behind.

The only comfort I find now is to continue these books, as you often referred to my lengthy texts. One day, I'm sure they will be compiled into a memoir from mother to son and perhaps passed onto Destiny for her son(s) if she ever would have children. Meanwhile, these memoirs help me to feel connected to my baby, my man-child, my son in whom I am well pleased.

I love that I had eighteen years to love you and nurture you. You were kind, and you cared deeply about others. You had the character to walk away from conflict, reaffirm others, lend a listening ear, and respect your teachers and those in authority. You were not wayward, troubled, or flailing. Your roots ran deep and your trunk wide and solidly planted so that even when life knocked you down during your father and I's divorce, you heeded the affirmation: *I bend, but I don't break.* I watched you go through that dark period of losing the closeness of your relationship with your father and still emerge from that hurt stronger than you were when it initially impacted you.

I cheered you on as you sought counsel from strong leaders in the community. You exemplified to other young men what to do when crisis hits and you find yourself at rock bottom. You started a support group to help other young men cope. I remember talking to you outside of the house in front of the garage on a day when it seemed our entire world was crumbling. We had a family meeting informing you and Destiny that a seemingly secure marriage of twenty-two years was ending. The security of our family was erupting, and the necessity of a divorce was most eminent. I spoke to you about your pain as you cried your heart out, encouraging you to find healing by helping other youth who shared similar hurts, and you did!

I watched you hit rock bottom from such devastation and then claw your way from the bottom of despair and redefine your life. I am so proud of you for your selflessness and unwavering love for your family and friends and for your strong sense of loyalty. It was your gift and your destiny.

With love,
Mom

PS: SPECIAL DELIVERY FROM MOM TO CURTIS ISRAEL GRAY on May 9, 2019.

CHAPTER 27

LONGTIME BABE

HEY, li'l guy! It's early morning, and once again, I can't sleep. I miss you immensely, and the lack of your presence puts me in a place of unrest. I went to go visit your grandparents. Granddad is not doing well; he is tired and longs for heaven. He says he prays every night that God allows him to wake up in "glory." I hurt for him, his condition has gone improperly treated because of sheer ignorance and lack of care. It annoys me, and I am doing everything I can do to help stabilize his condition. He is under wrongful care both at home and under medical professionals. Mom does the best she can, but her lack of knowledge on his condition is a direct result of misinformation from his doctors. I just don't understand that kind of blatant disparity. When you were too young to understand, I would communicate with you in this manner, often speaking over your head. Often, the dialogue was one-sided as you struggled to keep up.

Remember, as you were growing up, you would ask me why I used "big" words? You would say, "Mom, why can't you be like other moms?" I would then tell you it was not my responsibility to come down to your level but to raise you up to mine. I would challenge you to look up the words rather than have me choose a lesser word for you to understand. You hated that! (LOL) You would whine and say, "Mom, why can't you just tell me what it means?" I'm smiling as I am recalling those moments. Clearly, my parenting skills worked in your favor because you spoke very eloquently, and your articulation and understanding of comprehensive subject matters were far above your peers. You could hold conversations with professionals and not be intimidated. You engaged fluently with men in authority at all levels—from military to civil to law professionals. Your ability to handle conversations on their level was quite impressive. I'm sure it also helped that you were born to older parents and raised by a stay-at-home mom with expansive dreams for your future. I was raising a financial guru who dreamed of taking the finance industry by storm! You told me you knew you would be rich because you were going to make your fortune working in the stock market as a hedge fund broker. You had an exceptional knack for stocks and a healthy appreciation for entrepreneurial endeavors. Both your dad and I worked for ourselves, living out an example for you and Destiny of what hard work looks like. You were carving out your future.

You said to me, "Ma, I know I'm going to be great." Let me tell you what, son, you are great! I am making sure the legacy you left behind and the contributions you selflessly made as a community advocate are not forgotten nor will it ever be. I am so proud of the work you began here in Flagler County, Florida. I found pictures of you doing food drives to help feed poor and needy families. You helped with the little leagues, inspiring the little kids. I am told that in your honor, many of them want the #8 jersey now.

Also, I was watching ESPN3, and a dear friend of yours was wearing #LLC on his lacrosse helmet and I was informed that a nearby collegiate track team is considering changing their cross-country track-and-field jerseys to #LLC. Your team-mates continue to run in your name during competitions, some have committed to play football in your memory and many others find ways to honor your life and legacy in their academics because of you. You changed lives, son. A young lady contacted me, she said you would walk her home every day while you were both in middle school. Here is the text she sent me:

Good afternoon, Mrs. Gray.

I believe my friend texted you yesterday....

Back in July, I won a competition, and my focus for this year is on mental health in our

youth in Flagler County. I have been wanting to plan a mental health 5K and was wondering if you'd like to be a part of it. I knew Curtis very well (he actually would make sure I got home safe every day in middle school), and I knew how much he devoted to our youth.

I really think something along the lines of this would be very beneficial for our community.

Please let me know what you think.

I marvelled at her words: "I knew how much he devoted to our youth." Wow! That makes my heart so proud that your peers recognized your efforts in the community. Amazing! Your legacy has stretched beyond our sleepy little town. A 5K race took place in New York, and an attorney ran in your name. I know I shared that with you in an earlier communication. I want to thank you, son, for being a decent, responsible, and committed young man. The new principal at FPC is very impressed with the impact you left behind, and he has offered to work with me on future endeavors in your name.

Today, the superintendent is delivering a presentation in your name at football Sunday (you used to love going to those church events because they would have you give the scripture reading). Anyway, Coach is giving me your #8 jersey; let me tell you, boy, it is a size *medium*! Oh my gosh! You know I can't wear a medium. (Yes, I have to wear your jersey at this event. OMG, I need Spanx!) I kept telling you to stop wearing those "ooh baby" shirts, but you wouldn't listen to me. You needed a large! Anyway, despite all that, I will be proud to wear it even if all I get in it is my elbow.

Much love to you, my baby! I kiss your photos and talk to you out loud sometimes. It would be so cool if you could hear me. Perhaps, you can. Death is a mystery, one that no one understands except when they die. It is those that remain who will always be puzzled by the finality of death. Anyway, babe, that is a conversation for another time!

REMEMBER, I LOVE YOU BEYOND INFINITY.

With love,
Mom

PS: SPECIAL DELIVERY. ANGELS, RUSH THIS ONE, PLEASE.

CHAPTER 28

HEY, SONNY

TODAY IS the ninth of March; I began my journey back to Georgia on the eighth, well over twelve hours ago. I left Florida full of optimism and a sense of accomplishment for finalizing some details (or so I thought) there, only to come back to Georgia and find a boatload of mail waiting for me here. The business of death is time-consuming; I feel like I'm constantly on the clock without a break. I want to step away from it all and leave all the details and nuances behind. I am going to give myself permission to have one day of total nothingness (at least I will make an attempt at it). I will try my best to ignore the massive mail and not make the phone calls necessary to finalize important details that can't be ignored. This is more than exhausting; I wonder, *Will it ever end?*

I came into town with your auntie Judith and spent the day with her as she waited to board the Megabus to Columbia to go see Mom and Dad. I think she will bring Izear back with her (let your uncle Judah know). Also, I went to Destiny's job today. I haven't seen her since I left on the nineteenth of January. I missed her terribly and was anxious to get back to her. I want you to know she is doing well. She has a job she likes at a makeup "museum" she's always wanted to work for. She is adored by her coworkers, and she seems to radiate in this line of work. All in all, I believe that we will be okay, the family is surrounding us and supporting us through it all; and for me, the grief therapy is helping.

I felt a small sense of victory in solidifying the city's commitment to place your marker at the tree that was dedicated to you at your memorial. Having that closure helps me to focus on other matters that are still unresolved. I'm learning to celebrate small victories. I am also learning to channel my anger into Thanksgiving, and I will revisit my gratitude list again. It's important that the positives outweigh the negatives where I can find them. You are at peace, you have fulfilled your purpose, your legacy is remarkable and is remembered with graciousness by many, and you have made your mother proud in more ways than I could imagine. The stories of your impact reach me from unforeseen places and people. I chose to focus on those things and the significance of their value and meaning to help me get through the difficult times.

You are missed more than words could ever describe. I want to touch your face again, have you lay your head in my lap again, dance with you again, fold your laundry with you again, fuss over the lawn again, and decide which cereal to buy for you again. It sounds silly, I know, but I looked forward to picking out whatever cereal you felt you wanted to eat. I miss the small things, there are too many to name. I feel you should come visit me again like you did in my dream of you extending to me your hand as a message for me to rise up. I want to see you even if it's just for a moment. I don't feel it's too much to ask, so I'm asking.

Anyway, my baby guy, it is late; and finally, the lull of the long day behind me leaves me weary and longing for a deep, comfortable sleep. I will dream of you, my son. Images of you will flicker behind my closed eyelids, and I will remember you with all the love a mother could have for her missing son.

I LOVE YOU, SON OF MINE.

Eternally,
Mom

CHAPTER 29

THE ALL AROUND SPORTSMAN

GOOD MORNING, SON!

I woke up to the memory of you playing basketball under the streetlights at the community center. You would always ask if you could stay a little longer. You would ride your bike there before you got your license to drive. You loved playing basketball. That memory led to the memory of how you began surfing here not long after we moved from Port Charlotte. Boy, that was quite the memory! You came home with your chest all scratched up; for about a week, you ran around the house with honey dripping off your nipples, they were raw from the surface of the board. I said to you, "Why are you, the little Black boy from Atlanta, trying to surf with these little White kids from Florida who grew up around the water?" You did not care; you loved the water and wanted to surf and soon learned you needed a wet suit. Nothing stopped you; you became an avid swimmer. I recall the concerns I had about you swimming in the ocean because you were so adventurous, sometimes throwing caution to the wind so much that you would pretend not to hear us (me) when I would scream for you to come out of the water.

It brings to mind a particular time, you were on the beach with your auntie Candace, Uncle Ank, B. A, Adam, and your cousins, and a shark swam parallel to you. They were all screaming, "Curtis, shark!" You kept swimming because you weren't ready to come out of the water, but when you finally understood you were in danger, you couldn't get out of that water fast enough (LOL)! As you swam to shore, your cousin, Adam, ran into the water and pulled out the hammerhead shark that was swimming next to you onto the beach. It had been injured, *thank God!*

Son, you were the kid that all the other kids' parents invited to every venture because you were polite and often made those you were with mindful of the tone they took with their parents. You would say, "Hey, don't talk to your mom like that. That's not cool." The parents loved you for that and would invite you over often. I remember when you went yachting, I can't remember which family extended the invitation, but it was quite an experience for you. You described the yacht as luxurious and the trust bestowed to you a high honor. You said, "Mom, they just had lots of money lying out in the open, and no one seemed to care."

Then I said, "They probably wanted to test you to see if you could be trusted, to see if the little Black kid would steal from them." You said, "I don't know, but it was like pocket change to them."

You were so blown away by that. I felt proud that you demonstrated character, and the families of Palm Coast trusted you.

Remember when you tried your hand at lacrosse? You were labeled a natural, and the coach and his sons really wanted you to play. It would have been a great opportunity for you for a four-year scholarship, but you decided, on my behalf, that the game was too expensive for you to participate in because you felt the equipment and the trips were too much to keep up with. I have regrets about that now. You determined that I couldn't afford it, and you cut yourself short on a great opportunity.

Recently, I watched a friend play on ESPN3. He wears your emblem on his helmet and on his shoes. He plays every game for you! You guys were as close as brothers, and it's beautiful to see how they still honor you.

Somehow, you tried your hand at golf. One of your friends' parents invited you to World Golf Village, and you experienced the world of golf there. Was it Mr. Jim who took you golfing? (I can't remember.) I thought, *This kid has so many opportunities and experiences most kids his age don't have.* One of the parents (your second momma) was kind enough to take a group of you to Fort Lauderdale. Was it Fort Lauderdale?

I will have to ask her. Anyway, she bought your jet ski license, and that was another adventure for you. You had a blast. It is one of your fondest memories you shared with me of you and your friends together, it was mentioned at your memorial, remember? I'm sure you were there, observing everything.

You also loved to fish. You would go fishing with your dad on his boat, and you found a spot off the bridge on Palm Harbor. You enjoyed it and you were very good at it. You loved the water, spending as much time in water as you could. When we lived in Port Charlotte and had the pool, I couldn't keep you out of it. When we moved here to Palm Coast and your friends had pools, you were always hanging out at the pool, enjoying water volleyball. You often got invited to hang out at the Hammock Beach Golf

Resort and Spa with your friend's family; the attorney who wanted you to spend the summer in Italy with his family, the uncles, grandparents, and cousins really loved you like family. You really had an enjoyable well-rounded life, kiddo. You guys did bonfires, sang, swam, jet-skied, and surfed; and you were invited to hang out at Crystal Lake for glass boat riding. I think that was Paul's family (I can't quite remember).

You lived a full life, kiddo. The kids were lost without you this summer. You were the life of the party! Everything about summer evolved around Curt. I knew your absence would have an impact. The parents are telling me the kids won't leave the house because you are not here. Summer was different for Palm Coast's youth, and it was felt by all. The parents are still contacting me, telling what an impact you left on their kids. It's still very emotional for them (your absence).

I got up this morning, thinking you were such an avid sportsman, from water sports to the streetlight basketball hoops, lacrosse, volleyball, fishing, golfing, boating, running, and football. You coached, you cheered, you challenged, and you were also in band. You were everywhere, and that is why the hole you left behind is so huge! I'm glad you lived your life at maximum level. Some adults will never have these experiences, but you made a mark that can't be erased. You were a teammate, team captain, little league coach, and the coach's right hand. Almost every coach in Palm Coast has worked with you in some capacity in both schools and because you volunteered with little league.

You are amazing. I say "are" amazing because just this Sunday, the superintendent, Mr. James Tager, and his wife invited me to come to football Sunday at Palm Coast UMC (across the street from the library). Anyway, he wanted me to wear your #8 jersey (I mentioned this in the last text). I still can't believe how I was able to squeeze all my voluptuousness into that "ooh baby" jersey! Mr. Tager reminded me that it was in that very pulpit you had read the scripture Mark 12:18. He read it to commemorate you and the life you led. He spoke of your faith in God and the time you spent with Coach Rigney. I finally met Coach Rigney, he had such admiration for you. You allowed your light to shine among your peers, and you remained relevant. That is powerful, son. Absolutely powerful.

I am so proud of you. Remember when you would go off to school and I used to send long text messages, saying that I was proud of you. You always asked me why I couldn't be like other moms and send something shorter. you read them anyway and shared them with your friends. I am so glad I did. You had a chance to hear my heart before you died. I have no regrets as your mom. You were a beacon of light for this city. People keep giving me stories about the impact you made on their family.

Thank you, baby, for showing us all how to "be great."

With love,
Mom

PS: MISSING YOU. ANGELS, EXPEDITE THIS DELIVERY, PLEASE. Thanks.

CHAPTER 30

MISSING YOU AGAIN, SON

OKAY, so you got the photo. I will explain that in a few. Yesterday, two of your friends were together, they saw me leaving my favorite dining spot and reached out to make me aware they were there as well, by sending a photo of me as an acknowledgement. I love those guys! Anyway, one of the guys is bringing his baby girl to see me. I'm so glad because one of the realities for me is that I will never have grand-children from you. Sadly, that bullet took my future grand-children when it took your life. I deal with that reality all the time. By the way son, I mailed out thank-you cards after the funeral (about fifty to be exact). They went to the School Board, local organizations, churches, individuals, and groups that served or supported your funeral/memorial in any way. The community showed up huge for you. Every part of the community came to take a stand against violence in your name! The cards and prayers from grief-stricken folks are still coming in. The ricochet of that bullet hit every entity and every person in Palm Coast. Everyone felt violated.

Anyway, as I was texting you, one of your friends sent me a text, saying he has been thinking about me, and he is coming to Palm

Coast around the fourth of July and will stop by to see me. Your friends have all been checking up on me, and I am so grateful for that. I heard from one of your other friends the other day as well. These young men miss you a lot, li'l guy. I was in the garage and found a bag of all your old track shoes, it just reminded me how you literally ran into and out of our lives, gone entirely too soon. If I could just smell you again, have you bend down to hug me again, yell at you for sleeping so hard again, fuss about your future again, have you sing with me in the kitchen again, and, for the love of God, do one of those famous dances you did all over Palm Coast again! Missing you is an understatement!

I was surely looking forward to your career in the financial world. You became very suave in the area of buying and selling stocks. By the way, that stock club you started is still going on. The guys are talking about going into that field of study. Great job, babe! I think you would have done excellent as a broker. You got your financial gift from your granddaddy. He made us learn the stock market, and we had to read The Wall Street Journal daily and be able to tell him when he came home from work which stocks were good to purchase and which ones to sell. We had to know IPOs, blue chips, etc. Anyway, you got that gift and talent honestly.

As a matter of fact, I just made a little profit this month; my stocks just went up .90 cents a share after dropping a whopping $2.35 a share two years ago. I just rode the wave on it. Patience is the name of the game in the stock market for sure! Anyway, enough of that, about that photo with the patio furniture and cushions, if you noticed, they have changed to a solid red. A birthday gift (and "you need peace" gift) from my girlfriend in New York. You remember her, she was at the old house? Anyway, as it turns out, I bought Destiny a dog that had a lot of anxiety, which we were clueless about. That dog, poor little thing, ate up and tore up everything, including the cushions on the chair! He dug a hole in the screen, so now I share my sacred space with lizards. Take a good look at the photo, you will see one perched on the ledge. Hey, but at least it's not a frog, right? You *know* how I loathe those things.

Also, he (Ranger) dug up massive holes in the backyard and ate the lining out of my expensive grill to the tune of eight-hundred-dollars! He ate the container for my silk plant on the patio, ate the patio furniture, ripped the grill cover, peed Destiny's room, and chewed through all his toys! He set me back $1,500 in damages. Because of him, my expenses are through the roof! Remember how you begged me for a dog and I said no? I got this dog for Dee, and I am telling you, I had to take him back. He was costing me entirely too much money. I got him because I felt that since I didn't get you a dog, I should have. Wrong! No more dogs for the Gray clan. Destiny will have to get a dog she can properly train herself in Atlanta!

Well, pumpkin, I'm trying my best not to allow my feelings to stay parked on negative stuff. I am sending these texts because the tone is how we communicated in talks and texts. It helps me stay attached to you. I love you more than you will ever know. You are my son, my God-given treasure. I knew you were special when your foot was the first thing out of my womb. You came into the world feet first! The doctor was happy, he shouted, "I have a foot!"

And I shouted, "Where is the rest of him?"

Everyone in the OR chuckled, but I was serious. You took your sweet time entering the world, but you exited much too soon. I do miss you. I have been looking for positive ways to deal with this. I need direction. I need help. I don't know what I'm doing. I have never been this way before; the territory for me is indeed uncharted. It's unbearable at times, but you had a knack for keen listening skills. This is why I take my time to write what I'm experiencing daily because I know if anyone understands, it is you.

Hugs and kisses always. Remember how I used to kiss you all the time and love you all the time and you asked me, "Ma, why do you kiss me all the time?" I think you must have been around thirteen.

And I replied, "So you won't grow up to be homicidal."

You groaned and asked me why I always have to use big words. I told you kids who don't get enough love grow up to be hateful and turn out to be murderers. How ironic was that statement? A young man who received and *gave* an abundance of love was murdered by one who could only exemplify hatred.

Parents really should take time to love their kids, it paves the way their kids' lives will go in the future. I didn't hold back. I loved you and Destiny daily, I still do with Dee, holding her and kissing her precious face, and she is twenty.

In your lifetime, you were loved abundantly, son. It is the greatest treasure a man can have. I'm glad God gave you to me to pour that love on and watch you share it with others. I love you, babe, and there ain't nothing—no eon of time, dimension, galaxy, or space—that can keep that from happening! Perhaps, you should try to describe that to the angels. I don't know if they have the capacity to experience human love. Hmm…that's one to ponder.

With love,
Mom

PS: ALL RIGHT, ANGELS, YOU ALREADY KNOW. SPECIAL delivery from Mom to Curtis.

CHAPTER 31

MOVING WITH YOU, SONNY

WELL, baby, we are back home where it all began for you: McDonough, Georgia. We moved here February 2001. You were only six weeks old, and we relocated from Lake Butler, Florida, hoping for great opportunities for our family. Your dad and I chose McDonough because we felt it would be a great place to raise a family. It was. I feel that now that your body has been laid to rest, it was time to bring you back to your home. I saw Destiny today; she seems happy that we are here. We laughed together today, sharing memories of you and her watching *Boondocks* as a child and you finally learning the lyrics of the theme music and singing it repetitively over and over again (like you did with any song you learned).

I took her to breakfast and spent the best $34.91 ever just to watch her devour her food. She hasn't been allowing herself to eat since you passed. She felt your presence today, and she ate with glee. I'm grateful. I had mentioned to her over the phone this morning that I wanted to take you both to the mountains this fall for the holidays; it was traditional for my family—granddad, grandma, and my siblings—to travel to the mountains annually. I wanted to begin a new tradition with you both. We will still go, all three of us, just as planned. You in spirit, of course, but still as a family.

I felt proud of myself today after a considerably gruesome fourteen-hour drive. By the grace of God, I was able to keep it together. Why so long? Oh, well because I started driving at 5:47 in the morning, thus arriving in McDonough after six hours of drive time. In tow on that journey was a packed 20' moving van, leaving all the remnants of painful memories behind in Palm Coast, Florida. I had spent an entire weekend with friends and family, cramming all that mattered into both my moving van and my car. Yes, it was unnecessary, I know, but I allowed your auntie Candace to talk me out of the 26' van. If I had that, I could have made the move in one load.

Once I arrived, I unloaded the van of its contents into storage and set up my necessities with my roommate such as my bed, clothes, toiletries, and food supplies, but I couldn't rest. From there, I headed to Atlanta, caught a bus to Daytona, arriving at eight o'clock the next morning, and picked up my vehicle up from the house—our home. The one that made you happy, and the one that held the pain of your loss in its memory bank.

Departing was a bittersweet moment; I recalled the look on your face as you entered the house just one year earlier, smiling proudly as you picked out your room. You took ownership of our home, getting us all moved in properly and helping wherever needed. You brought all your friends there for refuge when needed, connection, food, and great times. I loved it. It made you happy; 4 Pringle Michael Lane gave mom and son a fresh beginning. It was there that you began to thrive; it was there when you embraced manhood on your eighteenth birthday. I felt it would finally be home, but that joy lasted only six months. We moved in the first of November; your life was taken six months later in April. God granted you six months to heal, become whole again, be happy, step into manhood, and find forgiveness for your father and a deeper relationship with your mother. Glancing in my rear view mirror as I pulled out of the driveway, I recalled all the moments; I let the tears flow freely as I drove, once again, toward a different destination back to McDonough, Georgia.

Anyway, it was tedious but worth it to get to your sister. She needed her mom; our loss was profound, having lost you and your father within an eight-month time span. She was spiraling, and she needed you and me to help her feel the support of family again. Her healing process is slow, but she is coming around.

As always, from infinity and beyond,
Mom

CHAPTER 32

I Changed My Mind

ON A BLEAK MORNING, I penned words of frustration—words of defeat and blame and anger—to you, my only son. Please forgive me for laying that burden on you. I realize that only I can change my outcome, only I can decide how I heal and remember you.

When you were about twenty-eight months old, I took you to the park, and you were having an amazing time, playing, smiling, and enjoying the swings and sliding board. It was a Tuesday; you looked up at me with those deep, winning dimples and continued to enjoy the whimsy of being a curious, active toddler. It was a Tuesday, and I remember the awareness that if something happened to me, you would not remember your mother. I prayed and asked God very simply, "If something should happen to me, would my baby remember me? Oh, God, please allow me to be the one to raise him up. Please allow me to be his mother at least until he is eighteen." I later changed that prayer to say until you were older and had children of your own, but something in me knew it would be until you were eighteen.

On that following Sunday, I blacked out behind the wheel of the car and went into a riverbed. They called me the miracle lady when I was rushed to the hospital because they knew there was no physical way possible that I should have survived that crash. God heard my prayer as I watched you play on the swings and run your little legs around the park. I made him a promise that if he would grant me the opportunity to raise you, I would teach you about him. I did. I prayed over you and your sister all the time that your steps would be ordered.

I asked God if death should ever come to either of you that he would not allow you to go without your soul being saved. He honored that request as well. I desired to raise up a man who would bring honor; once again, the request was granted.

Son, you are witnessing firsthand the goodness and mercy of God that has been upon you all the days of your life. I was angry with him; I thought we had a deal. I wanted more, but he gave me far more than I could have ever imagined. Your eighteen years mark a legendary life. Your name will live on because God made sure your name would be great, and he trusted you to represent him and be an embodiment of the greatness he placed in you.

I now release myself from the place of anger I had tucked away in my heart against the only comforter and keeper I know. How ignorant of me to fall for the lie! I know that it was the goodness and mercy of God that kept you as you lay there on that gurney absent from the presence of a mother whose heart has loved you with the fullest capacity a mother can have for her only son. He did not leave you lonely. He shielded you with his peace and blanketed you with love that only he could give. He comforted you in the midnight hour and protected your soul. He granted you an opportunity to forgive and release so he could receive you without blame into his kingdom. He assured you as you lay there that me and your sister would be all right. He spoke to you all the things you knew of him, and he revealed his truth in you. You were comforted in knowing that everything your mom had taught you over years was indeed correct. You asked me after all the lies had been revealed in our family, "Mom, suppose everything we believe is a lie?"

My response was, "Son, suppose it isn't? I admonished you not to gamble your faith on the flaws of a man. God is still God." Curtis, the sovereignty of God is without question. Even in my anger, confusion, and disgust at the loss of my only son, I could not deny the sovereignty of an Almighty God who has made me a promise I have believed since I was a small child that my children and their children shall be saved. For you, my dear boy, did not have physical children, but you have planted such a crop of seeds that only eternity will reveal the harvest. The young men you mentored are striving to make your memory count. They want to live a life of greatness to honor you and many of them will.

I have loved with full capacity in my lifetime, withholding nothing. I believe because of that God has rewarded me in ways that are yet to be revealed. I now know it was not in vain because you immolated that same love and dispensed it generously to others—an extension of my love and the love of God pouring out from you to others like an unending spicket, never running dry. You could not turn it off even if you tried; you loved even as you lay there, dying. What a legacy! A legacy of love is what you left in this little, sleepy town of Flagler, Palm Coast. You were and are an ambassador on assignment to show the love of Christ in a way that was tangible, relatable, and obtainable.

In my former post, I told you I felt that I had been shorted on love. I have not. I said I was depleted of love and have nothing left to give, but I do. My spicket does not run dry either. You and I, baby, are fashioned from the same love of God whose mercy is from everlasting to everlasting. I know you were concerned when you received my other letter. Forgive me in my moment of humanity. I will bless God with all that is in me, and I will show forth his praise.

Your sister is another vessel I must pour into; it is important that she is not left without hope or the assurance that God is for her. Her suffering has been immeasurable, and I know that God is holding her because he cares for her as well. You and her are both my best loves.

His blessings during all this tragedy are amazing to behold. I have decided, son, not to tarnish your legacy with anger but build upon it with thanksgiving and the memory of how beautiful your life was here on earth. Thank you, dear boy, for being relevant and not religious, for showing what relationship looks like, and for taking the time to love unfeigned, withholding nothing.

I am so proud of you and the man that you became.

Much love, Mommy

CHAPTER 33

LUMP IN MY THROAT

MY COMMITMENT to grieve for you pulls me into the very place I wish not to be. I have been very acquainted with its pull of persuasion as it usually manifests with a lump in my throat and tears that are impatient to free themselves from the traps of my eyes. They have been waiting for me this morning, my constant companions, the lump and the tears. They too feel the need to free themselves from the chains of restraint. They are restless most times, and they awaken me out of my sleep. "Free us!" they scream, and I obey. I release them sometimes until my body needs assistance. Sometimes, they are subtle and only require the backs of my hands and a gentle swipe across my face. Other times, they erupt without control, and I am left mercilessly to their timetable and their force. Often, the need for a sedative follows the impact it places on my body, my mind, and my torn soul. The ache also, on occasion, asks for release. I obey. I help it with music and the permission to remember your smile— the deep rumble of your laughter—your petulant pouting when you absolutely did not want to fold your laundry, and your crazy dip and sway and arm movements that became your signature as you did the "woe." Hahaha! Whoever came up with that crazy dance had no idea you would take it to a whole different level.

This decision to grieve you without restraint is for you so that you feel fully the depth to which you are missed by the one who birthed you. You must understand that the pain in bringing a child into the world passes as the stitches heal and the body mends. However, the pain of having to willfully say farewell to the same child that was birthed into the world with joy and expectation has no expiration. The void will always remain. The grave for a mother's child holds her precious promise and a piece of her soul. You were not buried alone; I too rest in the box with you. The Carmen that once was is no more. She has also laid her soul to rest along with her only son. A portion of me is in the box of your resting place. On April thirteenth was laid to rest a son and his mother, both inseparable, both carried into eternity.

Now, I who remain to occupy the earth must earnestly live a life that reflects an appreciation for the man-child that once grew in my womb. Carmen 1.0 is no more. Carmen 2.0 must learn life all over again, how to love and be loved, how to remember with wet cheeks and lumps in her throat and know that while, eternally, she will never stop missing you until you reunite, the grieving is her space to remember you with every fiber of her being. Carmen 2.0 is left to feel pain and anguish and must trust that it will only strengthen her for the journey ahead.

Carmen 2.0 is needed by the one child who remains, Destiny Amaris, your sister. She deserves a mom who chooses to heal and rediscover life in a way to be impactful to others in your memory and to honor the life she lives as part of your legacy. She deserves to be granted permission to mourn you as a sibling without fear that the raging waves of despair will pull her under without release. Grieving is essential for us, Curtis; it is how we cleanse the sting of your murder. It helps us to release the toxins of the violence associated with your death. Grieving is a mirror reflection of the depth to which we miss you. Therefore, the tears flow freely, forcefully, and the lump lingers longer at times more so than others, but I grieve because it is the measure to the depths of my love for my only son, my one and only male replica of me.

You, my boy, will never be forgotten. For all the many times I held your face and kissed you and breathed the words I love you on your neck, in your ear, squeezing you to my chest, I am so grateful that I never held back my floodgate of love for you and your sister. My capacity to love you was enormous, therefore, so is my grief. I used to tell you that my capacity to love was that of freight train as opposed to a thimble. God just created me to love enormously. You were indeed like me in that regard, loving all those that came in your circle. Your friends were blessed to partake in that gift; your ability to love unconditionally was truly a gift from God. You and I got that from your granddad. Now you understand why you grieved your uncle Judah so fiercely; it was because it was a direct measure of how much you loved him. I'm sure the reunion between the two of you is amazingly awesome. Give him my love and tell him I think of him often and I miss him dearly. He would be proud of Izear.

Well, my baby, the tears have stopped flowing, and I will pen you again. Go visit Destiny, she needs you. I love you, baby guy.

Eternally,
Mom

CHAPTER 34

RIPTIDES

I SIT HERE at the edge of the ocean's shore, willing the cool saltwater to come closer; my soul yielding to its inviting edge, soothing with foam, and the rushing sound it makes as it clashes with the beach. There is an overcast that is appropriate for the gloom I feel in the continued awe of your departure. I visited your grave today and consciously discerned (as a mother would) the barrenness of your plot, deciding if I should replenish the removed flowers and flowerpots with artificial plants that would likely need less attention. Suddenly, just like the force of rushing water, while speculating the decorative elements I'd like to place on your plot, from deep within erupted a riptide of moaning, wailing, and the infinite feeling of loss expressed in guttural sounds that can only come from the womb in which you once lay.

I left your grave site and traveled to the beach for healing, deep calling out to the deep, my baby, my baby, my baby! I call you, but do you hear me? Perhaps, if I send your name out upon the waves as they meet me at the shore's edge, they will take the whisper of your name back to you as a message. Yes? Without a bottle yet bobbing at the throes of the rashing waves, gliding above and beneath the ocean floor, your name, Curtis, whispered from a mother's aching heart through the passage of her lips. Son, can you hear me? I call for you. Then as if the waves feel the languishing of my heart, they meet me, surpassing the distance between me and the edge of the shore; flowing underneath my feet, they whisper, "We will tell him you are here."

Suddenly, gravity pulls the message back into the deep, but I know it carries your name with it. In sync with the salt-laden water of the ocean, the salty tears begin to flow down my face, and I respond to the invitation of the water for cleansing and healing. I now stand at the ocean's edge, waiting for the next wave to pull the ache out of my heart, and when it does, the strength of that pull lets me know, just like the riptide in my heart, the ocean floor has a riptide strong enough to pull me in, tugging, tugging, tugging until the tears are replaced with ripples of laughter as I recognize my vulnerability in this moment and in the ocean's wake. I know now that healing is taking place.

With love from the riptides of my heart,
Mom

CHAPTER 35

GOOD MORNING, MY RAY OF SONNY DELIGHT

YOU STILL THINK I'M CORNY, I know (yep, cause now you are smiling). Go ahead and admit it, you look forward to these letters. Anyway, I wanted to give you a heads-up, Ms. Betty passed, and I'm sure she will introduce herself to you and share with you our connection. I asked her to be your surrogate mom until I myself am able to embrace you, son.

So much has happened since my last letter. Today is the twenty-fifth of March; we and the world are faced with a virus attack that has taken many lives. Your uncle Sam was in the hospital, but he was released yesterday. They are calling this new strand of the flu Coronavirus or COVID-19.

If, somehow, you are permitted to look out for your sister, please do so. She will be in Atlanta alone. She insists on going back. Right now, we are in Florida, and she is staying with your auntie Candace, but I'm going to pack up today and leave.

Anyway, this letter is short. I wanted to let you know Ms. Betty may come see you, provided she made it to paradise. If she does, don't be alarmed and tell her I miss her and love her.

Love you, my one and only son,
Mom

CHAPTER 36

HEY, BABY, IT'S 2:45 AM

ANOTHER SLEEPLESS NIGHT, son, with thoughts of you running through my mind, bouncing in my heart, echoing out your name. I see your face, yet I can't touch you or feel you. I can no longer hear that bass in your voice. Nor can I stand on my tiptoes to kiss your dimpled cheeks. I want to clasp your hands like I used to, but the hands along with the rest of you have vanished. Your absence is a constant reminder that the lack of time is cruel and taunting. I loathe the absence of the space we shared together; it is empty now and obsolete, void and vanquished. I ache with the pain of your departure as though the gaping wound that was in your body now lies in mine; oh, how I would have traded places with you, giving you my years so that you could continue the legacy you began. A mother is used to laying down her life for her child. It begins with birth. There is no promise that the process of childbearing will be successful, but a mother gladly sheds the blood and lies in expectation of birthing a child into the world, knowing full well there is no guarantee that the transition will be successful, and no matter the complications, she will take that risk with each pregnancy.

I felt your father should have been the "Curtis Gray" to answer the call on that fateful night of April thirteenth. It should have been him lying in your place. It would have been understood, expected, and even noble. No one would have felt cheated nor would the sorrow be as tremendous. The loss would have quickly faded, and life would have gone on. I'm sure if given the choice, he would humbly agree. Nevertheless, heaven decided, before you were conceived, that it would be you who would depart on that day. I am still struggling with the decision because I was never consulted. Perhaps, it was determined that I would fare well with your date of expiration. If this is a test, I believe that it is one I am sorely failing. I don't have the confidence that my grade will be one that will bear the words, "Well done, thy good and faithful servant." I am missing the mark on this one, and I know it. I am struggling with the ability to find humility in my tone, my questions, my willful acceptance, and my obedience to know that this was indeed the best plan or outcome. Everything within me resists the urge to humbly accept this as God's will for *my life* or for yours.

Jesus prayed for Peter, "Peter, I pray that your faith fails not." Would you be so kind to ask him for me if he can include me in that prayer? Daily, I feel my faith failing. My prayer is that the one who made me will find the part in me that will eventually yield to his divine will for my life. I feel that your death has been my ultimate failure in which I will not find any recovery or solace. Everyone sadly pats my hand and tells me that eventually "time will cause the pain to fade." Perhaps, God will be merciful to me and allow me to experience it for myself; right now, the pain is raw, it rips through my sleep and stabs me throughout the day like a lethal wound that just won't heal. Perhaps, I need the antibiotics of peace and the medication of acceptance because the pills I am currently on mock me. They are a cruel form of deception, a non-antidote of chemicals that cannot medicate the space of the soul. The medication I've been prescribed cannot penetrate the layers of deeply embedded sorrow; it is a pseudo form of "aid" that lacks the ability to bring sleep and comfort the spirit of a torn mother's heart or, for just one moment, replicate peace. Instead, I am left with constipation and an earnest desire to escape this daily dose of deception.

Sonny, when you were troubled, I would lie in bed with you and pray over you to comfort your spirit. I would hold you until you felt your anguish calm down, I would rub your head and try to send comfort to your troubled heart with a gentle massage, always praying words over you to bring you healing and comfort. I need that now, and there is no one to hold me and comfort me, no one to hold my hand, no one to whisper words of encouragement in my ear. Although, I do know that people all over the US and abroad have been praying for me and your sister; it is indeed something I find comfort in. I now have to be deliberate in my own recovery because if I don't, my pain will turn rancid, seeping out bitterness, and thus tainting the beauty of your memory. I will not allow my pain to tarnish your legacy or overshadow your sister's future. I am determined to allow the bandages and salve of time to gently cover my wounds, keeping the contamination of anger and utter confusion from penetrating my heart. It is not fair to your memory for me to partially heal; the price that has been paid is far too great. I must fight to become whole and restored.

I will find ways to trust God daily. I know it is a choice. I will fight for ways to heal beautifully because that too is a choice. I will find ways to continue to live my life in celebration of a young man who once occupied my womb, leaving behind a trail of stretch marks to remind me that he resided there for nine months. I had to be surgically lasered to bring you into this world; my recovery from that procedure was slow because the stomach has seven layers (so I'm told), every layer needed proper time to heal. I was advised by your doctors and nurses not to try to do a lot of bending, lifting, pulling, or stretching. So it is the same with your death; I feel that, symbolically, your extraction from this life represented a lasered exit. Laser surgery uses fire to rip open the womb. It smells like burning flesh, and no matter how much medication you are on, you feel the effects of that procedure during and after the surgery. The lingering pain is like no other. I feel that the symbolism of your entrance into this world is an uncanny replica of your exit from it, ripping, searing, burning pain in which the recovery is longer and more extensive than a scabbled procedure. The funny thing is I would endure that pain repeatedly to have you and the joy your life has brought to me as your mother and the contributions you have made to the world. As you did with my belly, son, you left a mark that can't be erased.

There are some mothers whose sons have lived to see quadruple the years you were given, and they only left behind heartache and pain. You left eighteen beautiful years of delight, eighteen years of unspeakable treasure, eighteen years of unforgettable joy, kindness, comical memories, and precious times. God gave me compounded interest with you because your life yielded so much in such a short period of time. You were thoughtful, you cared deeply for others, you loved your sister with everything, you loved your dad, and you had a great relationship with him for most of your life. You loved your family deeply; you highly respected the men in your life, your mentors (you held them close in your heart), and valued their listening ear and guidance. You thought more of others than you did for yourself; even from a small child, you always put others' needs above yours. You were amazingly accommodating and self-sacrificing. Is it wrong for me to be angry that such a treasure has been cut off from my life? I try not to be, but it is difficult.

The beauty is that I've been blessed to have a daughter who's also reminded of your presence and who wants to make hers count in this world as well. You've inspired your sister; I believe that she will live to accommodate others' needs and provide humanitarian contributions with her life as well. One thing your father and I tried to show you both is how to live your life in a way that is pleasing to God and how to be good to your fellow man. I am glad I was able to see that play out in your life, and I am looking to see how it will play out in your sister's life. I find that this is the only thing that helps me deal with the pain of your short life span, taking into account all that you did with the time you were given, and I know it was not in vain. I feel cheated on time but not on the quality of the life you lived. I was blessed to have had such a child be chosen for me to raise, love, and nurture. I used to tell you all the time that you would live to be an old man; it was the hope that I clung to. I would tell you that your grandchildren would gather around you to listen to the stories of your adventures, and on the last occasion that I rehearsed this in your ear, one tear rolled down your cheeks, and you told me, "No, Mom." You knew you would not live to be old. You knew your time was close, but you just couldn't tell me because I was not trying to hear that.

You accepted your fate with the valor of a king. You knew that your time mattered, and you worked tirelessly to finish your course. I am pleased with you, my son. I am pleased. You made your mother proud. Joe and Vic said you would tell them all the time, "Everything I do, I do to please my mom." Son, you have exceeded all expectations. I guess now I must live my life to do the same for my father; please ask him to bear with me. This is difficult, and I still have to handle this pain. I can only do it with his help and guidance because right now, no doctor or pill can do the trick.

Baby guy, I have been writing since 2:45 a.m. The time is now 4:40 a.m. It's my therapy for healing. I do love you so much! Missing you is an understatement; I long for you daily, craving the deep rumble of your voice or that crazy laughter, your epic dance moves, our singing at the top of our lungs, and those super deep mother-son conversations. I treasured it all—every single bit of it. Thank you for being my son; I will always be grateful you were entrusted into my care.

I hope God is pleased with how I raised you. It was done to the best of my ability. I stood before him and dedicated you to him when you were barely six weeks old. He had had his hand on your life since you were in my womb. I trusted him explicitly with you then, and I trust him now to carry me through all this pain.

I love you, my baby, throughout all eternity. You will forever be my son!

With love,
Mom

CHAPTER 37

CHANGED POSTURE, SON

IT'S MORNING. I passed by the mirror and realized how definite my once squared shoulders and lifted chin droop. When did that happen? I find myself deep in thought, recalling the morbid details of November 19, 2017. It was the day of discovery that would lead to this place in which I find that the weight of that discovery has changed my posture. The deterioration went unnoticed due to the glare of blinding evidence of decay, trickery, and twenty-one years of arbitrary deception masked in subtle, miniature lies.

You, Destiny, and I's world erupted on what seemed to be a normal day. You knew a secret. You carried the weight of it since you were fourteen years old, caught in a web of lies by the man you revered. You were afraid you would be responsible for the breakup of our family, and you did not want to bring hurt to your mother. You had discovered the devastating truth about your father. How confusing it must have been for you to see him morph from an internationally sought-after minister, preaching all over the US and abroad. He was the same man who taught you how to serve humanity by feeding the poor, serving the needs of others, and engaging in the community. You always saw him lead, often giving out of his pocket to serve the underprivileged, supporting orphanages, going to Africa, purchasing cars for families without transportation, sending money to Haiti, and helping to feed communities. It was what you knew. It was what you were trained to see.

Suddenly, this minister became sinister, revealing his secret addictions. He remained functional, however, covering every step until you unmasked the truth. It changed your relationship with the man you adored. He couldn't risk you unveiling what you knew to me, so he lied and burdened you with the urgent need to become "the man" of the house causing you to believe his drug usage was due to terminal lung cancer, and the drugs were "prescribed by his doctor." By then, you were fifteen years old; and under this lie, your dad would often tell you he would not be around to see you graduate. In your sworn duty to "not tell mom, she would only worry," you carried a burden of lies no child should be subjected to. I couldn't understand how your GPA began to slide, and your cheerful demeanor was exchanged for anger and aloof indifference. You were caught in a web of lies that tormented you; I had no idea, baby. Mom is so sorry. I failed you. It was my job to protect you, yet the sociopathic behavior of the man you fondly called dad became your constant companion.

When you became seventeen, the bottom dropped out for all of us. The weight of all the years of deceit exploded, imploding upon you, Destiny, and myself. The sheer disbelief of what was happening caused me (us) to question everything. I checked your father's birth certificate to make sure his name was really Curtis Bernard Gray. Who had I married?

You changed your name to Curt, no longer wanting the association of a liar connected to you. You came to me fist clenched, pacing the floor, saying over and over, "I'm the son of my father." Tears flowing, you could not be comforted. I took you outside and held you; you were afraid that your life would become a mirror reflection of the deceiver who lived under our roof. When you had cried without comfort for as long as I would allow, I took you by the shoulders, pointed to the largest tree in our yard, and said these words to you, "You are also the son of your mother, and my roots go deep. You come from two lineages, son. My father, your grandfather is noble and honest, a giver, a man of remarkable strength, and a man of great character. He is a preacher who has maintained his integrity and has not compromised his family or his faith."

I encouraged you to lean on the men on my side of the family whose names held honor and valor. I then told you that the tree whose roots ran deep had just come through the worst storm. Irma had come through our county with a vengeance, yet the tree remained standing. I took you by the shoulders and told you to take a good look at that tree, to notice that while some leaves and branches had been ripped by the force of the category three winds, the tree itself remained standing. I told you that you were like that tree, that no matter how strong the force of wind of deceit, lies, and trickery, just like that tree, you would bend but not break. I said to you to repeat those words with me, "I bend, but I don't break." It became our creed, one I made you live by.

I have to admit, I must now repeat those words to myself; for a while, I was able to forge ahead and free myself and our family from a marriage whose facade was just that, a cover for which your father could hide his true identity. What I haven't been able to recover from are the many intricate tiny "breaks" along the way that have caused me to inwardly slouch. The burden of the weight of your death, its everlasting effect on your sister's life and mine causes me to bend. It manifests in my physical stance. I have to conscientiously pull my shoulders back, always aware that unseen to many is the enormous load that I carry, one that is too heavy for any human. My precious son lived his life to protect his mother when it should have been me protecting you.

Now as I pass the mirror, I see the slope; it started without notice. Even under the skillful hands of regular visits to the chiropractor, it is there. My body has confirmed to the enormity of the unbearable set of circumstances that is a reality from which I can't escape. You are not here. You are undeserving of the fate you suffered; you practiced what you were taught from a child, a life of service to others even more so to help kids like you who were tormented by secrets behind closed doors. You could relate to their pain, and you set out to make a difference, working tirelessly to rescue kids who contemplated suicide or whose life seemed reckless because of hopeless despair. You found them, you counseled them, and you poured yourself into their pain, admonishing them to "be great."

This morning, I recalled these things, and I pulled my shoulders back as my reflection glared back at me in the mirror. "I bend, but I don't break." I will hold this creed until my body believes it and reverses the slouch and the droop associated with the pain of your death. It is inescapable, a constant companion that desires to twist my physical being into a person I will no longer recognize, so I lift my head up and look at the face in the mirror, and I know that I cannot break because you made me promise you "I would be great." It is the reminder of that promise that holds me accountable to you, to us, and all that it has cost us.

This morning, I decided to change my posture.

Much love to you, my son, from here until infinity and beyond,
Mom

CHAPTER 38

SONNY

Missing you, my baby.

It's late, so let's chat in the morning! Much love.

I am packing so I can go heal. We have a lot of work to do, and I am often clueless about what to do next. I pray that God will lead me and guide me. I need his help. Anyway, I realized it's been too long since my last post to you. As you can see, this one is much shorter because it is very late (after 1:00 a.m.). I find myself getting in my car and driving around late at night, wandering around aimlessly because I don't know how to make it through the night without you. It is the most incredible feeling of grief ever. The feeling is like being lost, disjointed, and misplaced. My son whom I carried in my womb, who was a part of my very body, is now gone forever. I don't know how to accept that. I relive it every night.

I miss you, baby guy!

Love,
Your mama

CHAPTER 39

TEARS IN REVERSE THIS CHRISTMAS

SHOULD I laugh in your absence this holiday? You are not here. Should I dare smile and show my gap in all its glory this Christmas? You are not here. Should I dance and sway at the sound of music and the cadence of rhythm in your absence? You are not here. Should I unwrap gifts and exclaim over each one as they are unveiled in your absence? You are not here. Should I lie awake with giddy anticipation, imagining the look on your face when you pull your gift from underneath an imaginary tree without lights, ornaments, or even your gift? Oh wait! You are not here.

I will reverse the tears on my face, clear the lump in my throat, and laugh heartily, remembering you riding down the slope on a trash can lid in the icy snow on a cold winter morning, screaming with glee on a long backyard slope in our McDonough home in Georgia. I will reverse these sad, old tears and grin from ear to ear, showing my gap in all its glory, remembering the look on your face through all the years of dancing with you, my boy. I will angrily wipe away these tears that try to rush past my eyes while I'm remembering just last year you gave me a gift (very proudly, I might add), a Michael Kors bag from New York. You were so proud to present your mom with it. I was full of glee and a little prideful that this was your thrust into the holidays as a man. You had just hit that defining age of manhood, and instead of demanding anything, you gave. Yep, I must blink furtively, placing my tears in reverse as I remember my only son this Christmas. But try as I might, they (the tears) are forceful and more powerful than me.

I am weakened with emotion, raw and pure, strong and raging. Here they come now, my boy, they whisper to me that they are here to help cleanse my torn, aching heart. They are here to grant me some emotional freedom while remembering a boy, a man, a son who just 365 days ago, shared a special Christmas with me. The tears echo that I mustn't forget the fleeting moments and cherish every memory. "No need to put us in reverse," they tell me. "Your son knows that each drop brings cleansing and healing. We are the greatest gift this Christmas, not to be wrapped neatly with a bow or placed under a tree. Let us flow," they say ever so softly.

I yield as I sit on my bed. Racking, shoulder-shaking sobs erupt, and I cave, covering my mouth, hoping to stifle the guttural sound escaping my throat, passing my lips. I can't control it. Don't fret for me, baby; this too will pass. I let what is necessary flow freely, an expression from my heart. Each tear holds a memory, each tear tells a story, each tear calls your name, Curtis. The torrent is subsiding now, and my racing heart feels free. Free to remember you with all the love a mother can muster on a day filled with family, the echo of old movies playing in the background, the smell of your favorite food wafting through the kitchen, the occasional laughter from your uncle Ank, and the gentle banter between him and your auntie Candace.

Destiny is upstairs, dealing with her own emotions, and you, well you have a better glimpse than we do of the true meaning of this Christmas season. Yet, somehow, I sense your gentle presence, patiently waiting. I know you wish I could hear or even see you. I don't, but I do feel you. You are saying "mother" in the way you used to when you really wanted to make a point. I hear you, sonny. I know that even in your absence, I can celebrate the almost two decades of beautiful Christmas holidays I had. Would you please tell God thank you for me? I don't want him to feel I'm not grateful—I am. I am

THERE ISN'T A GIFT FOR YOU UNDER THE TREE, BABY BOY, but the gift of tears is an indication of how much your mama misses you.

Much love to you this Christmas, my boy.

Loving you without limits,
Mommy

CHAPTER 40

LITTLE BOY, WHERE ARE YOU?

IT IS IMPORTANT that you become my translator. It's simple: tell God I'm trying. I'm trying to worship, the words taste rancid on my tongue, they hurt my ears, they remove the scabs of wounds that are trying to heal. They remind me that he is sovereign, and his ways are higher than our ways. I wish he had fashioned me not to be inquisitive and demanding and confrontational. I wish that he had made me docile, a doormat that would lay down and just take shit. But since I was a child, I have fought everything. I don't know how not to. I fight the bile that forms in the pit of my gut because I have no answer for your death. I fight to withhold my anger from him and just accept what I cannot change. I fight the incredible weight of knowing that I am a woman who had never received love from a man and struggled to know unconditional love as a child. I ask, "Who marked me? Who decided that love in this life would not be my portion?" I listen to these songs of worship, I sing them, but I have never been a conditional lover. I loved God with everything my soul and spirit could give; I loved him till my soul was depleted. I held nothing back because his love for me was authentic. I still love but in portions, doled out in safe measures to make sure I won't have to live with continual disappointments.

When will it ever be time for me? I'm afraid to give my all now because I feel that I will be punished for that too. It would have been better had I never been conceived—never even imagined. I'm not sure what the plan was, but it has been filled with sorrows that are beyond normal. Insurmountable pains that seem to have no end. My love is and always has been the target of punishment. No matter who or how I loved, it had caused me anguish. I am like a turtle finding a need to hide within its shell for protection of impending danger. I am in retreat. I hope the love I gave was appreciated for it was without measure or limits, enough to spill over into my future to cover the deposits I now lack. Over the years, it has been interest-bearing and yielded much fruit, however, now I am barren and must wait for another season and harvest. I am done. I can't give anything else; my reservoir has run dry. You will have to speak for me; you must rehearse the words to God's ears that I spoke in yours for years for I have nothing left to say.

You are my translator, son, speak for me.

With love without conditions,

Mom

CHAPTER 41

TEXT FROM MOM TO CURT ON APRIL 29

LITTLE GUY, do you get text messages in heaven? *I figured with the satellites circling the earth, perhaps one of the angels could come into our spectrum and retrieve this message?* Just a thought. If so, this is your mom again, sending you so much love and beautiful thoughts of you, colored like the many colors on the color spectrum, reflecting hues of color for which earth has no description, colored with accolades for you, my young prince! This memorial for you yesterday I pray reached heaven. Perhaps, you and the angels were able to pull up chairs and pass around popcorn with front-row seats to watch the hearts of the community mend together as we celebrated the life you left behind.

I know that your father God will say in his loving voice to his prized possession with a smile and a twinkle in his eyes, beholding you with immense pride, "We'll done, my good and faithful servant, well done." You will then hear me say the same words, not with nearly such cadence and vibrato but with a personal echo, softly spoken and whispered in your ear just like I used to when you were troubled and I wanted your spirit to catch my words. I would place my mouth to your ears and whisper words to heal the hurt in your heart, words to exemplify my love for you, words meant for you and you alone from mother to son. I too would say just like God your father, maybe even a little misty-eyed, "Well done, mama's baby, well done."

Now the next chapter for me and your sister begins. I title this chapter *healing*. Today, I will make appointments for Destiny and myself to go through grief counseling together. It's time for us to mend. I can't serve this huge agenda you left behind without properly mending. It's hard to pour out precious ointment from a leaky vessel. It will spill, some will be wasted, and the value will be diminished. So it's time for me to mend, heal, and have my broken heart repaired from the loss of half of my treasures. I'm sure that God has a master plan for the surgery, post-op, and therapy of my heart. Once it heals completely, I will be able to function with you not being here every day, playing the music loudly, teaching me whacky dances. (By the way, I did the "woo" at your memorial, did you see it?) The kids were going bonkers! I could feel that smile of yours so contagious as we celebrated your memory with joy. Anyway, as I was saying a second ago, I will be able to accomplish the goal set before me.

This was your race, my baby guy. I used to tell you all the time that you ran in my belly, and when you were seven months old, you would run in your little walker! Those little, skinny legs would move so rapidly, and your little face would beam when your legs would move with the grace of a runner. Wow! Back then, I had no idea that you came into the world already knowing you would run, baby, and run you did with so much fervor.

I believe you knew that your life span would be limited because you were so compelled to accomplish your goals even when life knocked you down and erected some hurdles. You got up, you ran, and you leapt over your troubles, running with a goal to pass the baton to me, your mom, who's not as swift, by the way, and who's body is not built for the same type of race. However, the finish line is ahead, and I have the luxury to sprint in your honor, and sprint I will, son, carrying this baton and eventually passing it to another (your sister) who will then pass on to her children in your honor and they to their children. I am a legacy birther, son. That is my assignment. It began with you, and it will continue until God brings us all home.

Well, my sweetie, I got so used to sending you such long texts that I am sending this one hoping that this will somehow reach you. Even though you would complain about the length of the texts, you would still share them with your friends. I don't mind if you pass this one around in heaven. I'm sure I will send you more marked *special delivery for Curt sent from Mom with love.*

Loving you in exponential and inexhaustible capacity,
Mom

CHAPTER 42

HEY, MY BABY!

WHAT ARE YOU DOING? I miss you terribly! There is so much to share with you, but I have to go to sleep now.

I met with two circuit judges, two commissioners, and a few other people today, and they are very interested in your accomplishments. I told them about the 2019 champ award you received for your active contributions to substance abuse prevention and on positive mental health. So many officials have come on board and are willing to help to further the cause against violence. Your legacy is now in at least twenty states (or more). So many teens and little kids are following your story; it's unbelievable, the impact!

There are kids in other states aspiring to be like you. A former NFL football player said you did more in your eighteen years than he had done in his fifty-five. The county commissioner said the same thing. One of the circuit judges has been following your story and has marveled at the significant community contributions you have made. I am so proud to be your mom.

I always share your story, that you were a kid who brought himself from the bottom up. I want people to understand you were not perfect but determined to overcome. It is in this truth that other kids can be inspired that no matter what travesty life hands them, when they fall, they can get back up.

I love you, baby! I told you your story would touch thousands of lives. I never knew that the cost of such a contribution would be your very life. I miss you, but I have comfort in knowing you didn't die in vain and no one can erase the mark you left behind. You ran track, therefore, you understood the timing and accuracy it takes to jump hurdles, pass batons, and get to the finish line. It is a skill of agility, timing, pacing, measuring, and speed. That is how you lived your life, and I'm blessed to know that God's gift to me was to allow me to birth a runner. That was your ultimate calling for the race of life, and you ran it well. You crossed the finish line. Now we run for you (your sister and me) and a whole team of people whose lives have been forever changed in this little, sleepy town of Palm Coast, Florida.

I love you, son, and I'm proud to be the mother of Curtis Israel Gray!

With love,
Mom

PS: Angels, speedy delivery, please.

CHAPTER 43

CELEBRATING YOU, SON

HEY, PUMPKIN, I know I haven't written in the past several days, but I have been working on your foundation. I presented before the BOCC (board of county commissioners) yesterday, and today, I presented before the Flagler County School board. I shared with them how you were the recipient of the 2019 prevention champion award for your role in bringing awareness to positive mental health and substance abuse prevention. Way to go, baby! You were awarded a plaque by project AIM, project phases, project star, and the community rehabilitation center of Jacksonville, Florida.

The superintendent for Flagler county has been amazing. I want you to know that every board member wants to get on board any way they can. You are still leading, my beautiful guy! I love you so much, it's unbelievable how much I love you. It grows every day more and more.

I am going to pick this up tomorrow because it is late, and I need to get in the bed. Remember how I used to settle on the side of the bed, sitting straight up and fall asleep like that? You would come in the room, pick my legs up, put me under the covers, kiss me good night, and turn out the light. I miss that so much! I have no one to do that for me now. Oh, my baby! How I miss you so much! Much love to you, boy of mine. Your mama loved you and loves you with everything she got!

With love,
Mom

PS: Angels, special delivery to Curtis, please.

CHAPTER 44

HI, SONNY

THERE IS A CLOCK IN MY ROOM, its mechanical ticktock has an alluring sound that lures me to sleep nightly. However, every morning, my eyes fling open around this same time, not to a chime or an alarm but the steady rhythmic ticktock, and I know my eyes nor heart will find sleep.

Are you waiting for me? Did you ask God for an appointment with your mom, perhaps thinking eventually it would click, and I would know this would be our time to meet in the quiet of the morning? The gentle, constant reminder that time for us is no more except that I make time to remember you, to recall the subtle messages you tried to convey to me. You knew the clock was ticking against your life, but you spared me, Sonny. You didn't want me to worry nor did you want me to intercept or alter God's plan. You were willing to be extracted from this space in time for the greater good. God had a plan for you. He was gracious to lay it out before you, and you accepted his will. You knew it would cause you to be terminated. You spared me, but in your own way, you tried to say goodbye without betraying the trust he bestowed in you.

You were always my protector, holding things to keep my heart from breaking. When you were eight years old, you would not allow me to get the groceries out of the car. You screamed when you saw me fall outside of the Ross, thinking I was dead. You dreamed so many things metaphorically at the age of eight. I knew then you were my special baby, gifted to see what others could not. You had a conversation with God at the age of twelve, and you accepted your short life span with a matter-of-factness that it would be okay because you had already experienced death. There was no fear in it for you. When you were nine, you helped your uncle and your father load us up and move us to Port Charlotte; at the age of ten, you moved us from Port Charlotte to Palm Coast. You always watched over me and Destiny. Your dad raised you with the expectation that eventually you would be the man of the house. When we moved on to Prince Michael Lane, you were indeed the man of the house, and I didn't have to worry about anything.

You came into my room one night, laid across my lap, and, without words, conveyed what was in your heart. I didn't want to know, but as this clock is ticking, I remember the feeling now. It was a silent farewell. "Thank you, Mom, for being my mother. I love you with all my heart. I wish I could stay, and I hate to leave you." I know you are astounded to know that I would know this. I didn't want to know. We both silently exchanged our hearts that night. I rubbed your head and asked you what was on your mind; you said, "Oh nothing." But I knew better; your heart was heavy. You made sure all your friends knew, male and female, how much you loved your mom. You knew they would check in on me when you left. You were a smart, little cookie.

I wondered if you would come to visit me after your departure, but you have been visiting nightly around this same time. I get it, my son; you are here with me. The rhythmic cadence of this ticking clock assures me of your presence. It's steady just like you—constant just like you. It watches over me just like you, lulling me when I need to rest and waking me like clockwork each morning. This morning, I asked myself what I am to make of this, and I knew this would be my time with you, time to remember, time to reflect, and time to love. How I miss you, kiddo. I looked you in the face this morning, I saw you in my dreams, I had fallen, and you extended your hand to help me up. No words, just steady, calming strength and my hand in yours with the assurance that when I fall you will be there to help me rise again.

I'm using this time to accept the things I cannot change and to embrace the essence of your character. It radiates even in your death. Valor, honor, and protection exude from you even in your absence. Thank you for being my treasure and for being the prince that was lent to me for the span of eighteen years. Thank you for the symbolism of your consistency; I'm reminded by this clock that your presence while gone in the physical, remains timely in your death.

I love you, my baby!

You are not forgotten but vividly remembered.

Eternally yours,
Mom

CHAPTER 45

TURNING PAIN INTO POWER

GOOD MORNING, my son. Grief is a horrible weight. The opposite of grieving or mourning is joyfulness or happiness. I would like to trade this grief in for joyfulness of heart. The only thing that gives me joy is knowing that you are with the Lord. You held on to your relationship with God, and in the end, that is all that matters. That's all that matters. The quality of the life you lived involved a lot of good and bad, ups and downs, happiness and profound sadness. You were angry at times and gave up hope for a better life, but I wouldn't let you give up without a fight.

You were so transparent in your pain. I used to tell you to never suffer in silence, that even if you couldn't tell me, tell someone, and you did. You bared your soul to those you could trust. They (meaning, your peers) still marvel at how you could have been on the bottom, battling depression, and help them fight through their issues. You turned your pain into power. You refused to stay defeated and ensnared with anguish. Your coaches, your principal, Mr. Reeves, your guidance counselor, Ms. Trimmer, and the athletic director at Matanzas watched you fight to get back up.

They watched you pull yourself out of a dark hole and decide to improve your grades, improve your athletic ability, recover your body from weakness due to injuries, and transition yourself for a better future.

Pause.

Let me pick up where I left off.

Wednesday, June 26 (twenty-two hours later):

I have to tell you something, I have been struggling with your death. Yesterday, I went by a counseling office to possibly set up the much-needed grief counseling sessions for me and your sister, only to be put off by the nuance of bureaucracy, meaning since you are a murder victim, the State will take care of the counseling needed by me and your sister. Today is the twenty-sixth of June. You were mercilessly killed on April 13, and the State has dropped the ball. It seems to me that there seems to be a lack of necessary coordination for Flagler county on how to handle these types of protocols perhaps because up until now, this has seemingly been a sleepy, little town.

Your foundation will change all of that. That is my ultimate goal: to prevent another family from being put off due to severe lack of urgency, lack of knowledge, and lack of available resources. This is unacceptable on so many levels. Thankfully, despite all this, it just so happens that you and I and your sister "bend but we don't break." That is evidence of God's grace carrying us even in the face of the worst imaginable adversity, and while this is true, one thing I didn't tell you before is that bending is not pleasant, it will stretch you under the force of extreme pressure. It will make you release your resistance, and it will sometimes feel like you are about to snap. But one thing is for sure, strong winds don't last. They come in at incredible speed and force, but when the wind passes, if your roots are deep enough, just like a tree, you will remain standing. Sometimes, along the way, we lose branches and leaves, but the legacy of the tree remains for generations to come. You haven't lost anything, son, because your roots run deep.

In the community of Flagler, the kids are grappling with a way to survive your loss. A parent shared with me photos from Snapchat and social media of them, struggling daily at your grave site and at the site of the shooting, doing whatever they can to manage their pain. It almost crushed me. It felt to me like a panic attack from the sheer weight of knowing these kids are grieving without guidance or assurance. I wish I could gather them all in my arms and take the pain away; the enormity of it is beyond what the adults can see. They don't know the seriousness of this type of rend or tear in the mental psyche.

At this point, I feel helpless, but I must persevere because something has to be done. I am going to reach out to the counselors of Parkland and see what they did to assist their community. Palm Coast has no clue what they are up against with this type of mental distress resting on the kids or their families. Yesterday, I said to the office manager of the counseling clinic that their counselors should have been willing to come together pro bono to assist the community immediately after this happened. Collectively, counselors from all over the city should have been summoned to assist in some way to ensure that the children have help in coping.

This is something your foundation will work on because anything less than that is a system of failure in mass proportions. These kids will grow into adulthood with some type of dysfunction, becoming a society of dysfunctional adults, parents, husbands, and wives. I had a very candid conversation with the mayor, the county commissioner, the city manager, and other city officials about not being "reactionary" but "proactive." They are looking to me to develop a model. By God's grace and wisdom, I will, so help me! I'm at a place now where I can table my anger and listen to his voice for guidance and direction. This task is too huge to venture into without help from him. He knew this situation would come, and he also knew that you would be the seed sown in the ground to produce whatever harvest he has in mind for the many lives of the people you touched.

I want to tell you something, I understand now the tremendous loss you felt as a child from the deception of your father. We talked so much about the power of forgiveness and the importance of going through counseling to heal. I knew you had worked through it and were working through it the night you, your boys, and myself stayed up till about 3:00 a.m., talking about all of it. You were convincing one of them to go through counseling because through your own experiences, you understood the value of it. It was an intense but necessary conversation, and I shared with you guys then that dysfunctional parents tend to break their kids but not to be anchored to unforgiveness.

Well guess what? It is a process that I am having to walk through, baby, and it is not easy. Only God can help me with this one. This is too big for me, and I need help. I need help because it is more than I can do on my own. Somehow, babe, you did it. You found it in your heart to be free from the weight of someone else's fallacy. You exchanged that pain, disappointment, and anger for forgiveness.

It was apparent when the change came; your friends and I talked about it after you passed. We narrowed the timeline down to three months, and that's when it became apparent you were free. You started smiling again, singing again, enjoying life again, and planning for your future in track-and-field again. Even on the night of your murder, you had fellowship and dinner with the man you forgave again, your father. I'm going to follow your example, and now I must do the same. No one is worth my peace of mind or my soul. I have made the decision. I just have to walk it out, and that, son, as you well know is the hard part.

I'm sure you recall the conversation we had at the old house about how parenting is not a one-sided exchange. I told you that as parents we gain value in allowing our children to teach us as well. You taught me so much, and I am grateful. You taught me the value in developing great listening skills. I believe that is why over eight hundred people showed up to your memorial. You were incredibly gifted to listen, often minimizing yourself to accommodate others around you in spite of your own pain.

When the news of your death became public, the news anchor from channel six news told me hundreds of interviews had been conducted in Flagler, and they couldn't find anyone to say anything negative about you. The news anchor said he thought to himself, I have to see the mom. I made sure they knew you were not unflawed. What they didn't realize is that I was willing to not only teach you but be taught in the interim. Remember our spats? Oh my! Especially as you were approaching your eighteenth birthday! Wow, did we have our share of challenges, but we always came back to a place of mutual respect and understanding.

I was so desperately trying to prepare you for the rest of your life, but around 6 o'clock this morning, God made me aware that

I was preparing you for your eternity. In essence, I was preparing you for your departure from this earthly realm to your eternal home with

God. All the hours of conversation, prayer, discipline, and admonishment to forgive were all to qualify you for your transition from this life into eternity. I pondered this, and I came to the realization that God knew better than either of us. That if I had known this would be the outcome, I would not have passed the test.

We had six months to prepare, baby. For six months, Curtis, we worked on improving, spirit, soul, and body with a strong sense of urgency. Did you know? Did you sense that life was coming to an end for you? You worked tirelessly at making sure your friends were okay, assisting others and trying to save the one who was assigned to you. You must have known. You worked on improving your relationship with your sister, and the two of you became closer than you had ever been, sharing a language that you both understood. You laid on me all the time as though you knew your time was running out, lying in my bed, resting your head on my shoulder, giving me extra love, and craving time with your momma.

I felt it too, that something was happening on that Thursday. That same week you made me promise you that I would be "great." I am trying to be that for you, and I will, but I didn't know the price would be so high. I am weeping even as I am typing. I feel like I can't catch my breath! No mother ever wants the responsibility of preparing their child for death, but I would rather it be me than another. Many nights, I prayed over you, watching you as you slept, asking God, "Please keep my baby." I feel as though none of those prayers were in vain, but truthfully, I would have moved heaven to keep you here! But if I had to choose, I know that you resting in the arms of Jesus is better than a life of hell on earth. So now I understand some of the why, and I think this is the part of the grieving process where I transition into acceptance.

With unfathomed love,
Mom

PS: ANGELS, SPECIAL DELIVERY. GET THIS TO HIM ASAP, PLEASE!

CHAPTER 46

I Need Guidance, Son

MISSING YOU FIERCELY, but Mama's got her nose to the grind. I am working diligently on your website and getting the foundation up and running. Don't think I'm ignoring you; it's just so much to do in such little time. I have a lot on my plate. Not sure if I will have a roommate, and can I afford to stay where I am or do I leave to go to Atlanta and hang out with friends until I can get situated? So many people have done wrong by me through either willful negligence or sheer ignorance. I am pissed.

Anyway, I need to stay strong. All of this is very difficult to manage, and right now, I really need guidance, money, and support. Talk to God for me and ask him to show me what to do and how to do it.

I love you,
Mom

CHAPTER 47

TOTAL TRANSFORMATIONS

GOOD MORNING, son. I'm on the beach (you know I can't swim). Did you see me this morning make a conscious decision to heal? I sat in the water, and let the waves pull grief out of my body. I was smiling so big that a big wave passed across my teeth and down my throat. I gagged up saltwater; I felt it was symbolic of me spitting out and releasing the agony of your passing, a cleansing both inside and out. I was okay though, although I do feel the grit of sand in my mouth still.

Guess where I am? I'm in Titusville, the place of origin for all the pain we have experienced for the past year and a half, the beginning of the end. Isn't it funny how God would bring me back to the place of pain and mark it as the memorial for my healing? God is the master strategist, and nothing happens by chance. I know that you are probably able now to see how all the dots connected and why things played out like they did. I had to admit that the obvious demise of your death rested on the actions of your father. The decisions he made and the pain he fostered led us to a new location.

I sometimes think that if we had not ever moved to Palm Coast, you would never have lost your life that fatal night, but I know better. God has the final say on how and when we depart this life. Accepting that reality, however, has been a difficult part of this journey. But judging by the impact your death has had on the lives you touched in this area, it is apparent to me now more than ever that Palm Coast is where you needed to be to live out your purpose. So many lives in this city and in others have been forever changed because you were connected to people in those places. For instance, the friend you had for six years in California, his life is forever impacted because of your connection. I understand he wanted to come to the funeral, but I'm not sure what happened.

Anyway, I began this letter by letting you know I was at a women's retreat in Titusville, Florida. Initially, I didn't want to attend because of the connection this city has to your dad's best-kept secret. However, despite that, son, I'm glad I decided to come. I learned or rather am learning to heal through music, dance, releasing anger, painting, and water. When I first arrived at the retreat, I was extremely doubtful that any positive change would happen for me. My posture reflected that inner thought, revealing that I walked in feeling and projecting defeat. My countenance showed weariness. There wasn't any sign of light or livelihood on me. I didn't recognize it until I saw myself on a video, looking cold, withdrawn, dejected, and hopeless. This women's retreat was a transformation retreat, using butterflies as a symbolism of emerging from a broken place (a cocoon) to release their beauty in transforming from caterpillar to butterfly. The entire theme was built around butterflies. The speaker is a Better Life coach who uses her own life experience to help women heal after being broken. I needed healing from anger and the anguish of your death. So God, the master strategist, had a friend of mine to sponsor me because she and her sister knew this would be a fresh start toward healing for me.

On day one of the conference, the hostess placed beautiful stones in a narrow vase and cleverly demonstrated, until the vase is broken, the value of the gems that remained trapped in the vase. To illustrate this point, she wrapped the vase in a bath towel and used a hammer to break it. It was elegantly demonstrated by the speaker as she explained how God allows us to be broken so that he can collect the broken pieces in our lives and make something of greater value by turning what was formerly a simple vase into a wonderful masterpiece. Meanwhile, the gems that were inaccessible before are more accessible and exposed only after the breaking. Following such a powerful presentation, the speaker summoned me to speak to me privately and said that when a masterpiece is designed from broken pieces, the value of that piece increases. She told me that through my own brokenness, my value has increased, and I will help other mothers heal as a result of my own experience. Does that sound familiar?

Son, perhaps you recall when our family resided at Fortress Place? I spoke to you outside on the driveway at a time when you were upset over the breakup of our family, and I told you that although you were devastated by the deception of your father's life, there were other young men going through the same trauma, and you needed to take the pain you were experiencing and turn around and help someone else. You did that. Your friends talked about how transparent you were with the suffering you endured and the mistakes you made, but while you were hashing out your own problems, you always made time to help them overcome their issues. That made a huge difference in the lives of your friends.

They all watched you struggle yet give away support and a listening ear to help them in their personal crisis. They saw you as being transparent and authentic. Curtis, do you realize there are so many adults who are not that selfless and compassionate to be able to table their own suffering to help someone else? Some of the strongest people can make room for someone else even when their lives are a mess. What a gift and great treasure! And you, my son, were a man of great value to many young people, male and female, in this area and in places like California and other cities.

I love that you listened, and you executed. You are exceptional, and I'm proud to be your mom!

Notice: I will not refer to you in the past tense. You are (not were) exceptional still. The kids are meeting daily to gain comfort from one another at your grave site. It amazes me.

LOVE YOU, MY BABY. Tell your uncle Judah I said I love him and your granny and grandma and all the family.

With love,
Mom

PS: ANGELS, DO YOUR THING. GET THIS TO MY BOY.

CHAPTER 48

TRAVELING BABY

HI, my son. I'm in the ocean at sea, traveling to the Dominican Republic, aboard the Princess cruise ship. I was blessed to have this trip granted to me because the person who was to come could not make the trip. That person suggested that I come instead in his place. I am so grateful he did. The gentle buoyancy of the water has been better than any therapy I have received thus far, better than sleep aids, depression medication, and counseling. The water has been my counselor and my medicine, its gentle swaying disrupting the disturbing PTSD syndrome that robs me of valuable sleep and rest. I took a nap today for the first time since April thirteenth.

Tonight, aboard the ship, I attended a live musical performance that made me think of you. There was a musical score referencing angels coming to transition a soul. I dabbed my eyes, thinking of how you must have been in the presence of the angels in the last moments of your life because I saw the tranquility of unabashed peace on your face at your departure. I was once told by a funeral director that they could tell if a soul departs this earth in peace or turmoil by the last expression on their face. Your face was placid as if you simply slept and were at rest, my beautiful boy.

Did you hear me today as I stood on the balcony from my room and called your name loudly above the roar of the crashing waves? "Curtis Israel Gray," I cried. "Thank you." Thank you, my son, for the utter joy you provided in being your mother. Thank you for being concerned about me as you departed this world. Thank you for brooding over me and your sister, watching to make sure we are okay. Thank you for the love you carried without bounds for me; it has seeped from heaven and kissed the earth. I can still feel your heart; your love was deep and wide and unmistakable. You didn't withhold your heart; you loved deeply, often leaving yourself vulnerable and exposed. That love has covered so many people. That love reaches to me every moment.

It's important that you know I can feel you; you occupied my body for nine months. That bond doesn't diminish in your absence, it only expands. I am so glad I expressed my love to you not withholding anything, a touch, a rub, kind words of affirmation, many kisses, and sentiments. I have no regret, only that I can no longer physically touch you, my love, for you will never be held hostage to the boundaries of the physical realm any longer. It transcends time, stretches beyond the galaxies and homes like a beacon to where you are and surrounds you still. Nothing has changed; as a matter of fact, you are more aware now of how profound my love for my only son is. You have the ability now to sense this unlike anything you've ever experienced here on the earth.

Son, this is the story that will remain as a testament to your existence. Once upon a time, there was a mother who loved her only son enough to dedicate him back to God, promising to raise him up to love and reverence the one who lent him to her. This mother cherished her son, teaching him, grooming him, correcting him, challenging him, and shaping him into the man he became. The mother would lie in her bed and pray over her only son and knew that the lessons she taught him would matter, and that one day, those seeds would bear fruit as evidence that she had done what she needed to do to the best of her ability: to train her son up in the way he should go. She was constantly making him accountable to his actions but accepting his opinions as a developing and thriving young man. She grew to appreciate the nurturing exchange between mother and son and was very pleased with him. She deposited love into him so that he would have a healthy outlook on life, and that he would also love others. She taught him the art of leadership and respect. She watched him blossom. She had sown her dutiful seed into her only male

child—watered, pruned when necessary, cultivated, and protected him—keeping the soil nourished and maintained. The son worked tirelessly to make sure his mother would be proud of him. Using his unique tools and gifts to take all that his mother had deposited into him and share it with those in his circle of influence, he began to bud. One day, that son departed the life he knew, but his life had begun to germinate and reproduce from the seed that was planted. The mother knew this was evidence that his life nor her work was in vain.

"Thank you, Curtis Israel Gray," says the mother, sometimes, as a whisper or as a roar above the crashing waves. For she knows that he is her gift that keeps on giving. She knows he can still hear her and feel her love abound, defying the limits of time or distance. She knows, because his love for her is tangible, that he would be concerned about whether she would still be able to connect to him. She does.

This letter is my proof, son, that the ties that bind are never broken. You are and forever will be my son, my beloved boy, never forgotten and always remembered with the biggest love a mother can grant her child.

Thank you, Curtis Israel Gray, for being my promise, my love, and my only son.

With love,
Mom

PS: ANGELS, PLEASE RUSH.

CHAPTER 49

NOTHING TO EASE THE PAIN

HEY, Sonny, I drank too much. It's a habit I will not conform to as it only provides a very short-lived temporary escape, vodka and cranberry. I'm not impressed because here I am up at 4:04 a.m., doing what I do best, writing therapy. I've been staring into space now for about forty minutes, frustrated that the sleep that clung so heavily to my eyes after pulling on the drink in my glass has suddenly abandoned me as it does every night. Nothing prescribed in a bottle from the doctor and nothing poured in my glass disrupt the awareness that you are not here. My spirit rises dutifully looking for my son, longing for my son, pondering the mystery of your absence. I still do not understand.

Everyone wants to find their own comfort in my acceptance of your loss. My womb is empty; it tries to recall the warmth of your prior occupancy. My heart is empty; it knows that you have been ripped violently from it. My spirit is restless, daily looking for the missing part of me that is no more. I feel sorry for people who try to relieve their sorrows into frustrating temporary spells of escape, a mocking lie that renders nothing in the end, no peace, only destructive dependency. The poor souls then get lured in again. I imagine the pain for them is deep enough that perhaps they feel some escape is better than none.

We all have our vices I suppose; mine is the need to express, to pound it out in words. I find solace in talking, speaking, writing, creating, giving hope to others, and penning my thoughts. This is my lifeline to you. I know you get these letters from the heart of your mother. I know this because I simply asked God if he felt the need to take you, then this is the one condition he needed to meet for me. "Make sure my baby gets these letters," I asked him in a way only a mother can. He knew. I'm sure people there are wondering how you can receive mail in heaven. I feel a little smug, thinking about it. "You have not because you ask not." God is true to his Word, and we know he cannot lie, and that's why you are receiving these letters. Simple. Now you are smiling and probably shaking your head. Yep. I know.

Anyways, babe, yesterday, one of your friends sent me a little piece of artwork you did at Rymfire Elementary School. It sent me into a deep swell of sorrow and explosive grief. I was emotionally drained after seeing such a sweet rendering of your artful expression, so pure, so innocent, such a treasure. I saw your name on this little masterful creation, and my soul seemed like it was torn. Someone took my baby from me, and this is what I have left, an artifact that proved he was indeed here, proof that you created and smiled and laughed and used glitter, and you probably felt proud of that little piece of Picasso. I reached out to your former principal; I was clinging to the need to authenticate that piece of artwork that mysteriously showed up. I needed to hear his voice of reassurance, the way he used to reassure me when I would drop you off at school, that you were in good hands with him. I just needed to connect the dots. It blew me away, and I wasn't prepared. I'm going to make it a point to go see him before I leave Palm Coast (he absolutely adored you). Did you know he and I cried together on the phone when he discovered it was you who was shot and killed in front of the laundromat? I really needed to talk to him yesterday, it mattered.

You will be happy to know that my stay in Palm Coast has been productive enough for me to leave it all behind. I finalized all the legal, medical, and community details and loose ends that remained open. Your headstone should be arriving soon, and finally, your plaque for the tree that was dedicated to you has been ordered. I am waiting for the release of your phone. My desire is to put some space between me and the constant reminder of the pain that lives in this city in the wake of your absence. I am on a path to rediscovery and reinvention. I must find a way to live up to the promise I made to you to "be great." I can only uphold that promise from a place of wholeness and wellness. All my doctor's visits will be finalized on the eighteenth of March, and I will leave this place behind, only to look ahead to a future with you and your sister. You go where I go, son. You live in and through me and your sister. We have a lot ahead of us to do still, but mending is the number one priority for me and Dee. I am looking forward to the "better" that is ahead of me and to Jesus who is the author and finisher of my faith, not the vodka and cranberry (smile).

As always, I'm sending this with as much love as I can possibly send you, hurling it through the galaxies, navigating through the Milky Way, and making sure it lands right into your heart. Do you feel it? Can you feel the penetration of all my love bombarding its way through heaven's gates to get to its final destination? Trust me, God and all his angelic hosts are used to my behavior, it's okay.

I've been barging in like this for a long time; I'm sure they are chuckling, saying, "Ah, and here is Carmen again."

Love ya, ma's baby.
Eternally yours,
Mom

CHAPTER 50

UNCLE CURT

GOOD MORNING, sweetheart! I'm awake and purpose-driven. I have a meeting regarding your back to school stop the violence community tournament. I'm back in work mode and don't have time to mope. I also need to narrow the delay on getting your headstone. The kids are going to the grave site and standing over a three by five index card with your name on it. They don't care. They just want to be close to you, but I was embarrassed and wept when I saw that. So I will see how quickly that can be expedited. Also, the marker for your tree has been delayed, but someone is pushing that along for me. I told them I don't want the kids going to the place of the crime to mourn you. They need a beautiful place to gather. So, hopefully, that will be expedited quickly. I'm going to the mayor's office today. I have a meeting with the city commissioner this month and a lot must be done to create a haven for the kids.

On a different note, The baby shower is tomorrow at 6:00 p.m. I will be representing you there. They knew you were so looking forward to being the proud uncle. I will hold that precious little baby girl, and coo at her and tell her that her uncle Curt loves her. By the way, I was shown the group chat conversation you guys had the night you died, and was told how you were encouraging, and eager every step of the way. I am so glad your friend was blessed with such a precious little one, because I don't think he would have recovered from your death. He still struggles; they all do. Anyway, I I was happy to hear that you were FaceTimed and got a chance to see the baby shortly after she was born. I am so very glad because you were looking forward to being Uncle Curt. Remember you sent me a text saying you had to get a job so you could keep your friend's babies in diapers, and I asked you, "All three?" You said, "Yes!" That was too funny!

Anyway…I'm just coming back to this text (two days later… oops). I will let you know how the shower turns out. I wish you were here, but I will take pictures and hope that the angels can send them to you.

All right, pumpkin, loving you with everything I got. Nothing but love, boy, nothing but love.

With love,
Mom

CHAPTER 51

WORDS FROM MOM TO SON

ALWAYS BE the bigger persuasion in every equation. In other words, your influence to do what is right must be greater than your willingness to compromise for what is wrong even if the person who wants you to do wrong has more influence than you. Be willing to man up to say no even if it may cost you something: a relationship, an opportunity, position, things, or money. The universe has a way of paying you back with interest for the decisions you make whether good or bad. Always choose good. Never be the person who can be persuaded into doing, saying, or acting in a wrongful manner. Everyone is always looking for someone else in their life to be the bigger person. Make sure in life, you always remain the bigger person in whatever scenario life presents to you. Why? Because you are a leader, and leaders must always lead even when no one is watching and even when it costs you something.

Let me tell you something, son, in life, character and integrity are essential traits for without them, you have nothing. You can be extremely talented, and it will open many doors for you, but only your excellence of character will bring you honor and make sure those doors are never shut. You can see that playing out right now before you. Talent can get you where you want to go, but character built upon integrity, excellence, and honor will keep you there. That's the difference between being a past memory and a legacy that will outlive your mortal body. Let that be your life's goal because you don't want the children you will bring into this world to suffer for the choices you make. Developing excellent character is just like weight training. You have to work at it every day. Pretty soon, your character will operate on autopilot. You will be very comfortable saying no when you need to without compromise. Then the people around you will know that you are not a wimp and can't be bought. You won't be anybody's flunky or chump.

Your life is evolving, and now is when you begin to make the decision that will impact you for the rest of your life! Choose wisely, never feel pressured, take time to think, and you may have to say, "Give me a few days to think about that." Never make a rash decision, and always weigh the worst-case scenario out before you decide.

As always, I believe in you, and I like you. I like the person you are becoming, and I'm prouder of you than you can imagine. You are becoming a version of your best self! Every day, you are stepping into a version of your best self. Never settle for less than that, and you will see amazing opportunities come your way!

Loving you with everything I got,
Mom

PS: Nothing but love, boy, nothing but love! (This letter was written to Curtis on October 2018, six months before he was shot and killed.)

CHAPTER 52

I Affirm You

GOOD MORNING, my son! Today is a new day for you! Celebrate your future and all the great things that are ahead of you. Make a commitment to yourself not to look back and embrace all the good things that are headed your way!

You are strong. You are resilient.

You are brilliant, and you shine.

You are a champion because you have already overcome more than most.

You bend, but you do not break, not now or ever. You are determined not to be a victim.

You conquer because you are a dedicated winner.

You are an overcomer! You win, and then you win, and then you win again.

You always get back up! You get knocked down, but you always get back up!

You are strategic. You are perceptive. You are analytical. You are appreciative. You are considerate, and my son, you know how to love yourself. When you love you, all the other trivial stuff in life has to respect the authority that loving yourself provides.

You know you better than anyone else, and you have evaluated your strengths, and you are working on your weaknesses. That makes you an overcomer, an achiever of great things, and a profound leader. Those boys you had at the house really respected you. You led them in this move, and they gave all they had for you because you led them. I heard them talking about you when you were in your room.

Boy! I was proud; they gave you nothing but respect.

You are a profound leader, and I'm proud to call you my son!

Last thing, regarding yesterday, it has no power over you if you don't give it power. Observe it for what it is. If it does not benefit you, discard it. You don't have time or energy to lend to stupid stuff. Just keep your head up and always look forward!

With love,
Mom

CHAPTER 53

IT'S 4:12, BABY GUY

YOU'VE BEEN with me all night—running—running in my dreams. First, in search of me, we were separated; I asked you to wait as I went in search of God only knows what. Curiosity led me down a winding road; night was fast approaching. I stayed too long. You were patient at first, then you began to sprint in my direction on that long road. I had turned around and was making my way back to you. My pace increased as I made your form out in the dark. Mother running to son, son running to mother, we connected and ran back together to the place of our original designated location. A sense of urgency binding our efforts to reconnect. You asked me in a tone of relief and agitation, "What were you doing?" The dream is muddled now, only fragments I recall. Somehow, this reconnect led me into another phase in which I found myself on a path once again, unsure why; but this time, it was daylight. It seemed that the path simulated a track field perhaps? I'm not certain, however, there were people on either side, but in the middle, as though doing a solo halftime performance, was a woman in a beautiful red blouse, golden skirt, and arms extended up as though ready to perform. I watched in fascination as she began to glow: her hair, golden; her skin, golden. She saw me as I neared her, turning her attention fully to me. She winked as her face began to glow, and the shimmering essence of her seemed transparent and radiant. From the hem of her skirt upward, she began to fade; I fell, covered my eyes, and began to wail. I knew she was an angel. The way she locked eyes with me, winking with a knowing secret, transmitting to me you were well. I felt disappointed that I could not ask the words, and that she was my messenger, sealing the reality of what I already knew, you had transferred into a realm from which it was necessary to send me a message from this glowing angel, a woman whose gentle assurance affirmed your departure.

Morphing, the dream changed again; this time, a younger, athletic lady waved at me from the sky. I cannot tell other than I was looking up as though through a portal; quickly, she began to fade. Not again! I thought. I found my voice and courageously yelled as she waved and smiled, "Is Curtis okay?" She smiled so brightly, then she looked as though giving you permission to show yourself, and in a flash, you too were there with her, very eager to put my mind at ease, beaming, waving, fading just as quickly as you appeared.

Suddenly, as I continued to journey through this series of dreams of you, you were there, standing taller than me, looking down at me as you so often did. I took the pad of my thumb and lovingly smoothed the silky thickness of your eyebrows, I smelled your skin, I laid my face to yours, and I nestled my head into your neck. I laced my fingers through yours; my baby guy, you were sent to me on loan through the portal of my dreams. The last time I felt your skin, it was cold, but your face was beautiful as though you were simply sleeping. This time in my dream of you, warmth greeted my touch, the scent of your earthen skin hit my nostrils, and your silky eyebrows glided smoothly underneath my thumb pad once again, a gesture I fondly used on you often to express my love for my Curtis, my baby guy.

Son, do me a favor, please. Thank those two angels for me and let them know they are welcome to visit me anytime. I won't be afraid because I know there is a portal for us to rendezvous in times when the heart of your mother longs for her only son. I had words for you. They escape me now, but you understand the words I love you. You'd heard them multiple millions of times from my lips to your ears even when you were in my womb. They have echoed in the courts of heaven, reverberating against the golden streets, bouncing through the pearly gates, running through the corridors, an earthly mother with a heavenly message sent to her boy. Nothing, no eons of time, separation of galaxies, dimensions, or even eternity can take that love away. It's powerful; it finds you like a homing beacon, spirit to spirit, from the womb to the tomb. The mystery between mother and son was enough to warrant the attention of angels and open heaven's portal, and so it is for me. I recognize the powerful pull of that love through God's amazing love for me, searching for me, finding me, waiting, and appreciating that his relentless pursuit of me and my acceptance of that pursuit gives me access to you beyond the earth. He loved us both enough to reconnect us in a way that only he can. Please tell him thank you. Remember your manners.

Well, we spent quite a journey together; it woke me out of my sleep. I needed to record it so as not to forget, my beautiful boy. Thank you for searching for me. I miss you too, my baby. Until next time…

Always loving you,
Mom

CHAPTER 54

GET UP, CARMEN

IT STARTED off as an inaudible whisper, "Get up, Carmen." The message was muffled in the nuances of daily existence, a sequential shuffling of my life on autopilot, drowning out the near quiet command, "Get up." Other noises interrupting the frequency of that directive seemed to echo loudly, reverberating and clashing into my former place of peace. My bearings were shifting, and the ground under me seemed to give away. I was falling, tripped up by trauma, and the impact left me lying still in a heap.

"Get up, Carmen." I lay there uncertain if I could or would ever move again; my insides were drained from the many convulsions of tears and indescribable agony. Someone needed to pick me up because this time, I just didn't have the strength nor the desire to fight. It seemed like every time I rose, I was being knocked down with greater force. I could feel myself caving into the weight of that reality. Why try?

Trauma sludges through my being, slowing down my momentum, my drive, my purpose, which now I'm not even certain what that is anymore. If I lay here, I will not be confronted.

Or will I? Perhaps, I can shrink within myself and just be, albeit it seems simple enough, yet I cannot find contentment in that thought because it is interrupted with the force of three words, "Get up, Carmen!"

At a time when I felt stronger than I do now, I cleverly wrote a book on the five stages of grief, revealing the process of grieving as has been outlined by many experts. However, since then, I have encountered a force, perhaps another dimension of grief for which the description can be adequately summed up as numb indifference or maybe even apathy. I haven't a clue how to fight that nor do I possess a weapon or tools to conquer it. My fight is gone, my strength is hibernating, and my will has taken a long vacation. I packed up all the tears I have cried and have placed my sorrow in storage. I feel nothing, so I lay here unable to get up. I just don't know how.

When I was fighting, I had a target, however, now there are illusive shadows, and I'm too tired to throw a punch at something I can't identify. I lie still because there is nothing else to do. Then suddenly, through the noisy trauma, I feel the words pull me to my feet; and shakily, I stand, knowing that I must rise. Strengthened by this awareness, I submit to its prompting to get up in spite of the pain, get up even when it hurts, get up even though I'm not sure of my next steps. But I do know for certain I cannot lay here, too much is at stake. It ain't over; it can't be. The cost has been too great for me to yield now. In truth, too many unfulfilled promises must be kept, and there is still work to be done. I don't have the answers, but that is not my burden to carry nor is it my responsibility to know what I don't know.

However, while I don't know what lies ahead, I do trust that when I fall, the spirit of God will raise me up. I am tired, even weary, abandoned in love by my husband, and the loss of my only son and two brothers. Tragic is what comes to mind as I lay out these losses before me; they seem to engulf me like tidal waves. I know that I am under observation by others as they shake their heads and muse to themselves inwardly and out loud to me, "I can't even imagine." Sometimes, I feel the pity coupled with wonder stowed away in their glances, wondering as they look upon me, How is she able to handle all this? It's a question I believe was reserved for the one who created me. Only God himself knows how much I can bear, and only he knows when the weight of sorrow will be replaced with joy.

I realize, lying here the uncertainty of anything is not an option for me. I must get up so that the death of my son is not in vain. I must get up so that the sacrifices of my brother, Samuel, don't fade away. I must get up because my mother has lost her way, and I want to be there for her when she returns home. I will get up because a love lost doesn't mean I will never be the recipient of true, unconditional, timeless love; in my lifetime, I will have that. I must because I gave it (timeless and unconditional love) without hesitation. I must get up for those on the sideline who have counted me out with empathy as they ponder my next move, wondering all the while, Will she throw in the towel now?

Truth be told, I have no towel to throw in, no white flag, and no "yield" sign. It's just me, rising to a standing position with hands raised in a simple gesture, "I yield."

COURSE WORKBOOK

A GUIDE FOR PARENTS WHO LOST A CHILD

Carmen A. Gray

www.longlivecurtis.com

EPILOGUE

Let the Healing Begin

HI, I'm Carmen Gray, the mother of Curtis Israel Gray, a young man of eighteen years old who was gunned down on April 13, 2019. I know the pain of loss and grief in the worst way—murder. In my tumultuous introduction to grief, I felt as if I would never breathe again, and sadly the thought was welcoming. I discovered a portal of hope—my pen. It kept me from losing my mind, my voice, my focus, and my instinct to thrive. I pray, dear reader, that you empower yourself through your own journey of grief. May both the book and the accompanying workbook serve as a guide for cognitive therapy that will allow you to journal as well.

GONE—A GUIDE FOR PARENTS WHO HAVE LOST A CHILD. The workbook is designed to help you navigate the process of healing on your own terms.

In my book, Gone, a guide for parents who have lost a child, you will recognize the stages of grief: denial, anger, bargaining, depression, and acceptance. By the way, there isn't any order to these stages, but they continue to cycle like waves on the water, sometimes placid and calm, other times raging. Analyze them and allow yourself the opportunity for healing post the loss of your child by giving yourself permission to grieve through the entire process. By the way, I hate the word process because in death, it seems ambiguous in my journey to recovery. This workbook, however, is designed to help you navigate the process on your own terms. Many people, in a genuine effort to comfort you, will gently state that you must go through "the process," but they themselves cannot relate to the heart-crushing anguish that is inescapable and redefining your life through loss.

However, dear parent, you have the power to decide how the death of your child will define you.

You will need to read the recommended chapters listed in the table of contents with each module. These chapters are also in the heading of each module for proper completion of the workbook. ***Happy journaling!***

This workbook will serve as a guide with printable tools to help you navigate through the grieving process. Please note that my only PhD is in LIFE. I am not a professional, only a mother who has learned to find a way to cope with the most profound loss of my one and only son. I needed help and could not find anyone to help me with resources or tools, so I am sharing the lifeline I created for myself, and I hope that it helps you in your journey of grief. I would urge you to add grief therapy and mental health care rendered by licensed professionals as you find ways to redefine your life because there will be days ahead when your desire to thrive will diminish through guilt, immense pain, and at times hopelessness. My Gone workbook is just a tool and cannot serve as a substitute for professional help. Find a support group, psychiatrist, grief therapist, or mental health coach to help you as you continue to heal. I did, and these professionals became my tribe.

Carmen A. Gray

1 MODULE 1: DENIAL

Coming to grips with the loss of a child is especially difficult because it defies nature. Recognize the signs of denial in this module.

2 MODULE 2: ANGER

Anger is a powerful emotion during this phase. In this module, you will find ways to *release* for total healing.

3 MODULE 3: BARGAINING

Bargaining is a symptomatic sign of extreme grief. In this module, you will learn to recognize and manage it

4 MODULE 4: DEPRESSION

Depression has many ways it manifests, and everyone is affected differently. Take time to deal with depression in this module.

5 MODULE 5: ACCEPTANCE

The timeline for acceptance varies. This module will provide goals for acceptance. To get to a place of acceptance you must have a plan.

6 MODULE 6: REDEFINING NORMAL

The loss of a childforces one to create a newnormal. Create goals for dealing with life after loss in this module.

7 MODULE 7: MEMORIAL BUILDING

How will you memorialize your child's life? This module includes a planner to help you structure a memorial.

8 MODULE 8: STAY HEALTHY

Grieving takes a toll on the body. Staying healthy is essential. This module will help parents plan for health post the loss of a child.

9 MODULE 9: RECOGNIZE TRIGGERS

Functioning blindly after the death of a child can be detrimental. This module will help you preparefor triggers as you go through the grieving process.

10 MODULE 10: IT'S OKAY NOT TO BE OKAY

This module will help you identify your tribe, havea system for purposeful healing through journaling, and allow space and time to not be okay.

FILLABLE PRINTABLE YEARLY CALENDAR

**Print the calendars and use the following chart
to gauge where you are in the stages of grief.**

Be aware that these stages are not in order and some will last longer than others,
and that is okay.
This chart will help you recognize where you are in the your healing process.

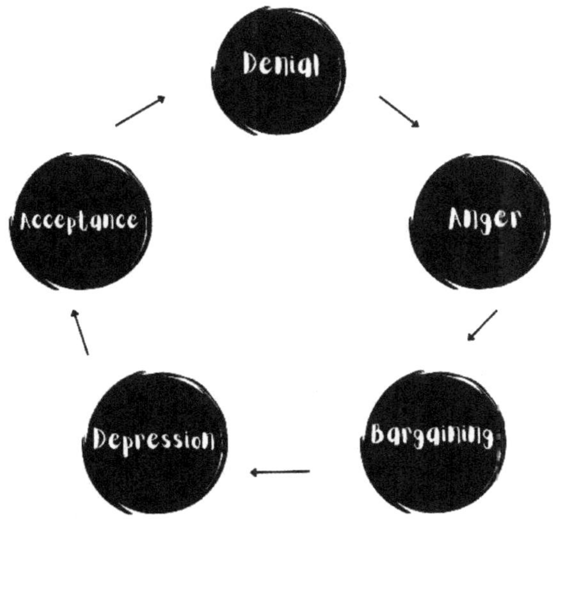

D = Denial   A = Anger
B = Bargaining
DP = Depression
AC = Acceptance

FILLABLE PRINTABLE YEARLY CALENDARS

January

MON	TUE	WED	THU	FRI	SAT	SUN

February

MON	TUE	WED	THU	FRI	SAT	SUN

March

MON	TUE	WED	THU	FRI	SAT	SUN

April

MON	TUE	WED	THU	FRI	SAT	SUN

May

MON	TUE	WED	THU	FRI	SAT	SUN

June

MON	TUE	WED	THU	FRI	SAT	SUN

July

MON	TUE	WED	THU	FRI	SAT	SUN

August

MON	TUE	WED	THU	FRI	SAT	SUN

September

MON	TUE	WED	THU	FRI	SAT	SUN

October

MON	TUE	WED	THU	FRI	SAT	SUN

november

MON	TUE	WED	THU	FRI	SAT	SUN

December

MON	TUE	WED	THU	FRI	SAT	SUN

MODULE 1:
DENIAL

I was in the courtroom with my son's killer on November 22, 2021, and shockingly he spoke with empathy when given an opportunity to make a statement. This was vastly different from the plea hearing, held on August 13, 2019, in which the defendant was angry and raging and his words to the judge and those in assembly were acidic and filled with hatred as he spat out, "F—— you." Since that time, 923 days had passed, and the tone and words were empathetic. I was not prepared. He pled guilty, and for all the things I did not want to face, suddenly they were there before me, and I was not emotionally equipped to handle it. My insides felt jellied, and I trembled incessantly as the reality hit me that all this time I had been in denial about my son's finality in this life. Somehow, I thought that along the way in my healing, I had come to a place of acceptance. This turn of events—a hearing, a plea, a judge, and a courtroom— somehow made this nightmare that I had been living in my very present reality. How did I not know that I was not prepared to face this enormous fact that indeed Curtis was not coming back? I was in denial and didn't know it. I could feel myself crash.

MODULE 1:
DENIAL

✹ Denial manifests when conversations, frequented places, and certain memoirs of the departed child are avoided.

✹ Choosing not to speak of the child in the past tense.

✹ Difficulty in departing with items such as furniture, clothes, etc.

Use the space below to pinpoint your recognition of denial:

____

____

____

____

____

____

____

____

____

____

MODULE 2:
ANGER

Anger is the dominant emotion usually interwoven with the other sectors of grieving. It is forceful and the depth of its penetration must be managed because it can cloud one's judgment and guide one's actions. If carefully managed, that anger can produce something good from the tragedy of loss. Often, we see that in laws being changed to benefit many through the tragic loss of one. Recognizing anger begins with honesty and a willingness to deal with it.

In this module, we will explore an effective way to deal with anger by writing letters of release. Perhaps you are angry with your child for causing such heartache. I find this is common after a child commits suicide. Perhaps you are angry with God for allowing this tragic thing to unravel in your life. In the chapter titled,"Little Boy, Where Are You?" you will feel my anger with God as I was not able to even pray.
Give yourself permission to unveil the truth of all those who are subject to your human emotion and write that person a letter. You may have to write more than one letter

Dear _________________ I am angry because

____

____

____

____

____

____

____

MODULE 3:
BARGAINING

In what ways have you used bargaining through your grieving process? Do you recognize them? Use the box below to write them out. Writing things down aids in seeing and managing the emotions and psychological energy of grieving and is considered cognitively therapeutic in the healing process.

____

____

____

____

____

____

____

____

____

____

____

____

"46 MINUTES"

Bargaining is a measure used to control the outcome. A parent will replay the events leading up to the death of their child and try to reimagine a different outcome "if only" or "I should have" or "what if." The bargaining or mental negotiations may be to change the outcome or change the timing of death. This part of the grieving process is tormenting because the mind wants to will a different outcome. It will replay the inevitable one thousand ways to either pause, reset, or rewind death.

MODULE 4:
DEPRESSION

"HEY, BABY, IT'S 2:45 A.M"

Now it's time for real talk on the subject of depression. What is clinical depression? According to the RTOR webpage (n.d.), clinical depression (major depressive disorder) "is more than just a temporary feeling. It is relatively long-lasting, can get worse over time, and significantly interferes with a person's daily activities."

Because of the violent disruption of murder resulting in the death of my only son, my diagnosis included the following: *PTSD, manic depressive disorder,* and
anxiety disorder. However, one could not look at my outer appearance or demeanor to even detect my diagnosis. I remained groomed, articulate, and seemingly stable.

However, my internal body was breaking down. *I had a team of doctors working with me because the impact affected my body.*
I experienced broken heart syndrome that manifested as a physical hole in the heart. I had two large tumors in my back that had to be removed and a rectal bleeding disorder that led to surgery. This brokenness was internal and could not be detected by my appearance. I was not unkempt in any way, and my face did not show signs of stress.
I lost 33 percent of my vision and struggled with unbearable pain throughout my body that could not be penetrated medically. Depression related to severe trauma should never go untreated.

Recognizing depression is the first step to recovery. In the boxes on the following page, list your symptoms.

MODULE 4:
DEPRESSION

Use the spaces below to list your symptoms of depression. Be sure to include emotional, physical, and mental traits that you recognize.

MODULE 5:
ACCEPTANCE

"HI, BABY GUY"

When grieving loss, acceptance can be tricky because it can easily be mistaken for being okay. Acceptance brings one to a place of understanding that the death of one's child is final. Often, the reality of the loss is the hardest part to grasp because there is a part of us that wants life to remain the same as it was before the death of a child. Many parents will feel survivor's guilt and try to maintain the "life" of the child without facing the reality of the child's death. **Use the ovals below to identify the mile markers you have used or intend to use to get to a place of acceptance.**

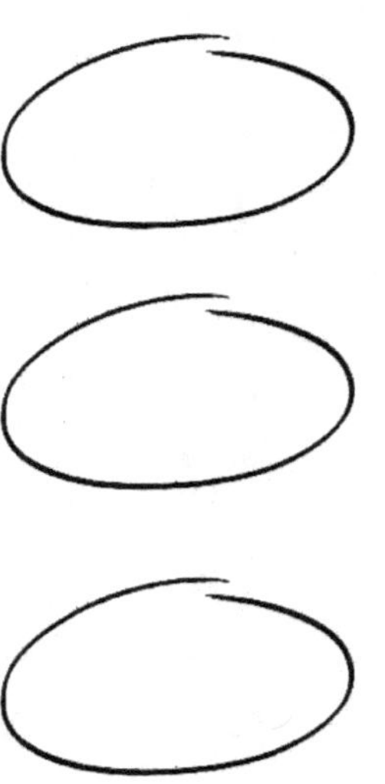

When I Think of Death
Maya Angelou
www.whatsyourgrief.com

" I can accept the idea of my own demise, but I am unable to accept the death of anyone else.
I find it impossible to let a friend or relative go into that country of no return.
Disbelief becomes my close companion, and anger follows in its wake.
I answer the heroic question 'Death where is thy sting?' With 'it is here in my heart and mind and memories.' "

MODULE 6:
REDEFINING NORMAL

"BROKEN BUT BETTER"

How do we move past the guilt of living life without our child? How do we redefine life when the natural order of life has been disrupted? Our children are to bury us, not the other way around. How do we move past what is not normal and find a new normal as a parent? The emotional turmoil of rediscovery post-death requires focused intention, and it begins with a decision. How will you honor the memory of your child and not be swept under the raging pull of guilt for leaving him or her behind? Redefining normal is difficult to navigate without a plan. Use this module to develop a plan for living past pain and using the pain as a platform to honor your child.

In your own words, what does a new normal look like to you? Use this space to jot down ideas, intentions, and a plan to move forward. Refer to the question above as a guide.

MODULE 7:
MEMORIAL BUILDING

In the "brain dump" below, jot down some ideas of how you would like to memorialize your child. Jot down ideas until something sticks.

"celebrating you, son"

How will you memorialize your child? It is an important sentiment to mark the life that no longer remains. What do you want to remember, and what do you want others to know? Death is a transition; however, the life of the departed is worth celebrating.

I was asked to attend a "rock ceremony" for my son. It was a trigger for me, and I could not enjoy the ceremony. Curt's death was just too fresh. The essence of the ceremony was for the victim's family to paint a rock that represented their loved one. I was insulted that my son's life was reduced to a stone. It took time for me to appreciate the representation of the memorial. When I had more time to analyze the value of the memorial, I built a rock garden for my son at home so I could see it every day.

MODULE 8:
STAY HEALTHY

Trauma impacts one's physical, emotional, and psychological health. A healthy state of mind is often dictated by our mood. Use this chart to gauge your daily emotions. When a parent loses a child, it takes a while to heal. Allow yourself permission to feel all the emotions you need to feel. Find a place that is secure and comfortable to grieve. However, as you are processing grief, have a goal in mind for your recovery and work toward that.

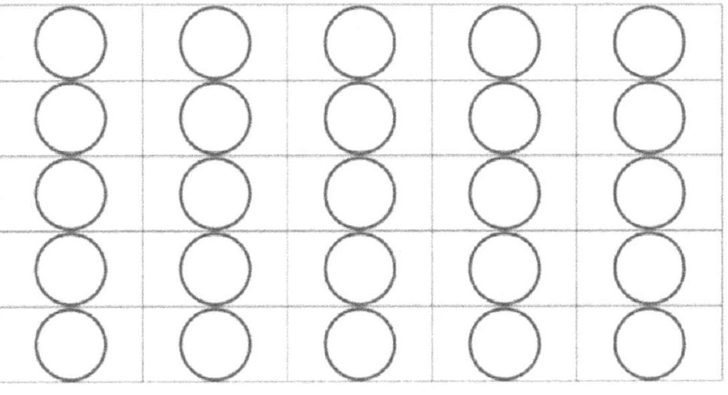

MODULE 9:
RECOGNIZE TRIGGERS

"CHANGING POSTURE, SON"

Recognizing your triggers is like identifying allergies. If you are not aware of what triggers your emotions, anything and everything can seem like a free fall. Being cognitive of the thoughts, sounds, feelings, smells,
places, and psychological episodes that contribute to feelings of helplessness, anger, pain, and distress is a powerful way to develop emotional resilience
so you can function in day-to-day activities, holidays, and special events surrounding the loss of your child.
Use this space to freely document each trigger as it surfaces. Please be aware that awareness does not eliminate the trigger; however, it does empower
you to manage the outcomes.

Use this space to write down **_a plan of action_** to manage your triggers. Examples include "talk to a therapist," "attend grief support," and "work on cognitive therapy" (this includes, dance, weightlifting, and group therapy). When you take time to write things down, it engages the brain to carry out the very thing that is documented. Thoughtful intentions are ineffective without an actionable plan to execute them. When you write down your plan of action, complete your follow-through in writing. For example, "I will attend group therapy on Monday, November 18, at 6:30 p.m. at XYZ Group Therapy for Grieving Parents."

Writing the thought down without an actionable plan of follow-through is setting yourself up for failure. When you have accomplished the intended goal, recognize the accomplishment in writing as a means of gauging your healing process. Healing after the loss of a child is a difficult and daunting task, and the reality is you will be in the process of healing for years to come.

Action
Plan

Execution
Date

MODULE 10:
IT'S OKAY NOT TO BE OKAY

"NOTHING TO EASE THE PAIN"

When I was going throught herapy, my counselors came to the same consensus: "Carmen, you want to rush through this without feeling anything." I felt that I would never feel anything else but the all-encompassing weight of grief and anguish and that I would never laugh again or smile or feel happiness and mirth. I looked for options to dull or numb the experience, and one day I realized that going through grief is the only way to get to an emotion I was not well acquainted with release—genuine release without guilt or regret. The only person you need to be transparent with in this process is you. Use this space to identify any vices along with an action plan to free yourself from them.

VICES

ACTION PLAN

....

....

....

....

....

....

....

....

About the Author

Carmen A. Gray is a sought-after keynote speaker and trainer with over twenty years of experience in the US and abroad. She has developed several creative workshop platforms over the years and has hosted many conferences to drive intended results among attendees looking for measurable outcomes in personal growth and leadership development. Ms. Gray is not a stranger to the public eye; she has been featured on many platforms in local, national, and global news and has served in community outreach initiatives through the local church and other endeavors both in the US, Africa, and Haiti. She's traveled to seven different countries with a broad acceptance of people, diversities, and cultures.

Ms. Gray is the mother of two beautiful children, Destiny Gray and her slain son, Curtis Israel Gray, whose life was violently taken on April 13, 2019. As a result of his death, Carmen founded the non-profit organization, LLC Rise Above the Violence, Inc., in her son's name that will serve communities impacted by violence through a prevention program to educate communities and their youth on positive mental health as well as how to heal in the after math of a crisis. In memory of her son, Curtis Israel Gray, and the ultimate commitment Carmen made to him to "be great," a slogan he coined and held her to several days before he died, Carmen has combined her creative talents with her strong leadership skills to spearhead the effort to be great in his name.